Praise for TORRENT OF GRACE

"It is of great importance that the church hold training and education in safeguarding and abuse prevention among the highest priorities. Mark Joseph Williams' generous and ongoing commitment to strengthening this essential work is a blessing for bringing Jesus' strength and healing to those who have been abused—as well as their loved ones."—**Bishop Luis Manuel Alí Herrera, Secretary, Pontifical Commission for the Protection of Minors**

"Mark Williams relied on the 12-step adage 'we are as sick as our secrets' to become a survivor. His courage and vulnerability were only possible with God's help. This is a grace-filled book that offers the church an opportunity to 'touch the wounds'—which is where the point of compassion begins."—**Jean Heaton, author, *Helping Families Recover from Addiction***

"What Mark Williams endured is so terrible that you may hesitate before starting this book. How Mark Williams found his way through it all is so consoling that you will never regret finishing his story, nor will you forget it. Torrent of Grace is for anyone who wonders whether there can be hope after the worst trauma possible—hope for themselves, for their faith, for loved ones grievously wounded and shamed. Mark gives us a powerful answer."—**David Gibson, director, Center on Religion and Culture, Fordham University**

"Raw experience and the honest disclosure of the long-lasting pain of abuse, pervade this work. Alongside, the rhythm of scripture beginning each chapter and the prayers interspersed throughout the text, indicate the depth of faith and the struggle for life that have marked Mark's journey."—**Gill Goulding CJ STL, Regis College, Jesuit Graduate School of Theology at University of Toronto**

Torrent of Grace

Torrent of Grace

*A Catholic Survivor's Healing Journey
after Clergy Abuse*

Mark Joseph Williams

ORBIS BOOKS
Maryknoll, New York 10545

Founded in 1970, Orbis Books endeavors to publish works that enlighten the mind, nourish the spirit, and challenge the conscience. The publishing arm of the Maryknoll Fathers and Brothers, Orbis seeks to explore the global dimensions of the Christian faith and mission, to invite dialogue with diverse cultures and religious traditions, and to serve the cause of reconciliation and peace. The books published reflect the views of their authors and do not represent the official position of the Maryknoll Society. To learn more about Maryknoll and Orbis Books, please visit our website at www.orbisbooks.com.

Library of Congress Cataloging-in-Publication Data

Names: Williams, Mark Joseph, author.
Title: Torrent of grace : a Catholic survivor's healing journey after clergy abuse / Mark Joseph Williams.
Description: Maryknoll, New York : Orbis Books, [2024] | Summary: "A survivor traces his path from trauma to healing to seeking an institutional path to the Catholic Church"—Provided by publisher.
Identifiers: LCCN 2024028499 (print) | LCCN 2024028500 (ebook) | ISBN 9781626985964 | ISBN 9798888660522
Subjects: LCSH: Child sexual abuse by clergy. | Catholic Church—Clergy—Sexual behavior. | Sexually abused children.
Classification: LCC BX1912.9 .W38 2024 (print) | LCC BX1912.9 (ebook) | DDC 282.092 [B]—dc23/eng/20240711
LC record available at https://lccn.loc.gov/2024028499
LC ebook record available at https://lccn.loc.gov/2024028500

Dedicated to
Rev. Monsignor George T. Deas
1925–2023
Friend and spiritual director for a half-century

"Love is holy because it is like grace—the worthiness of its object is never really what matters."
—Marilynne Robinson, *Gilead*

"All power in heaven and on earth has been given to me. Go, therefore, and make disciples of all nations, baptizing them in the name of the Father, and of the Son, and of the Holy Spirit, teaching them to observe all that I have commanded you. And behold, I am with you always, until the end of the age."
—Matthew 28:16–20

Contents

Note to Readers

This book includes scenes depicting child sexual violence and child physical and emotional abuse, which may be triggering for some readers. Sensitive topics such as self-harm and addiction are also explored. Reader discretion is advised. If you experience any discomfort or distress, please seek immediate professional medical advice.

Foreword

Jennifer S. Wortham

In the evocative pages of *Torrent of Grace*, readers are invited into the intimate and profound journey of healing and transformation undertaken by Mark Joseph Williams. As a courageous survivor of clergy abuse, Mark openly shares the deep scars left by his traumatic past and the challenging path to recovery that followed. The narrative poignantly captures his struggle to reclaim a faith that was deeply shaken by the betrayal of a beloved priest and how forgiveness has played an integral part in his healing.

Throughout this remarkable book, Mark articulates the nuanced role of spirituality in his life post-abuse. He describes how his once-damaged faith, a source of immense pain, gradually transformed into a vital tool for healing, imbuing him with a renewed sense of purpose and resilience. He also addresses the practical aspects of his recovery, underscoring the importance of professional counseling, community support, and the therapeutic power of advocacy and speaking out.

Mark's journey, which is still unfolding, resonates deeply with my own experiences both as a survivor of child sexual abuse and as the sister of two brothers who suffered at the hands of our parish priest. We met while I was leading a global initiative to establish a world day for the prevention of and healing from child sexual abuse. Mark joined our team and swiftly became a trusted advisor and key contributor to the establishment of the United Nations World Day for the Protection of, and Healing from, Child Sexual Exploitation, Abuse, and Violence. I have grown to deeply admire his unwavering commitment to the cause and his indomitable spirit.

Torrent of Grace is not merely a story of personal triumph; it serves as a profound educational narrative, illuminating the often overlooked emotional and spiritual wounds inflicted by abuse. Mark stresses the importance of a supportive network and the need for institutions to create environments where survivors can seek help without facing stigma. More than a book, *Torrent of Grace* is a compelling call to action for societal change and a poignant reminder of the indomitable strength of the human spirit in overcoming adversity.

Let us all be part of this journey, in the hope that together, we can build a future where such stories are no longer common, but relics of a less enlightened past.

Jennifer Wortham, Dr. PH, leads research on moral injury and the impact of religion and spirituality on health at the Human Flourishing Program at Harvard University. She is Founder and CEO of CoreSensum, focused on transforming the delivery of mental health care. An award-winning activist, she is recognized for founding and leading a global collaborative to establish the November 18, United Nations World Day for the Prevention of and Healing from Child Sexual Exploitation, Abuse and Violence.

Prologue

For the many people harmed by abuse, there is no greater pain than the feeling of shame. And in many instances the shame we carry isn't even ours to carry, instead created by those who exploited and used us. This is something I know well. When I was a child, I was sexually abused, first by a teacher and then by a Catholic priest.

Carrying that kind of trauma is the devil. It stays in the core of your being. For many victims of abuse, they go to their graves never revealing what they endured. For fear. For shame. Some— like my friend also abused by a Catholic priest—take their own lives because they cannot live with that unbearable pain.

In my own life this torment of shame took many faces: addiction, depression, suicidal thoughts, bankruptcy, job loss, and home loss.

A line was crossed. My childhood was lost. My development was stunted. I was afraid. I did not know how to break away. When trust in another was broken, brokenness took root in me.

My life became so fragile and grew into severe isolation. I was young when my father died at only forty. My mother responded by falling into rage, loneliness, and drink. In my early life she was largely absent. By her late thirties she was a widow and would live only to sixty, dying not long after I married. Looking back at the circumstances of my life, I was prey, vulnerable to being groomed for abuse.

The kind of pain I endured and the shame I carried weren't,

as I later discovered, rare. The Church's crisis today stems from large-scale, ongoing sexual violation and abuse at the hands of priests, and it is a crisis that threatens the heart of the Church and its sacredness.

The depth of this crisis is unfathomable: priests have sexually violated children, minors, and vulnerable adults, including seminarians.

For far too long the Church has tolerated this harm. Truth didn't seem to matter. Secrets abounded. Files were concealed. Priests covered for other priests. Abusers were moved to other parishes who weren't informed, and then the cycle of abuse began again.

But those who were victimized never forget.

For me, the saving grace was my healing journey in grace itself. God's loving grace somehow reached me, and in that grace I found my ultimate spiritual director in the person of the Holy Spirit. My story of grace also includes religious women, family, friends, and the surprise of some good—flawed and holy—priests, human like all of us, bonded together by a loving Christ—all who were people who heard my story and never failed to love me.

And yet, at first, none knew my secret—the same secret that the hierarchy of the Church kept for far too long.

Within the silent secret the Church held, it was difficult to for me to find my voice. It took time.

Now we are meeting a watershed moment in the life of a broken Church. No time is more pressing for all to learn to weep. Bishops—including the Bishop of Rome—must now weep. At this writing, in the historic time in the life of the global Church, during the Synod on Synodality—a time set apart to listen to all brothers and sisters in and out of the pews and discern how to enhance the fruits of meaningful communion, participation, and mission so as to walk together as pilgrims of faith, the

Church must listen now to the voices of those it has most hurt through its devastating silence, neglect, and selfish self-interest: the victims of clerical sexual abuse.

People are leaving the pews in droves. And Catholics will not continue to embrace a hierarchical Church if those appointed to lead will not encourage healing, insisting rather on holding onto the false power of clericalism that exonerates abusers and those acting to cover up their sins. It is only by forgiveness and refusal to exonerate those who harm the vulnerable that we can shape a renewed community of believers.

No longer can the Church ignore the collective voice of the abused.

To truly imagine a different Church under Pope Francis during and beyond the Synod on Synodality process concluding in October 2024 requires what Ronald Rolheiser calls "paschal imagination," for those hurt sexually by the Church, for the journey from victim to survivor where a real theology of healing is found in the lived experience of those, like me, who have touched a living death on earth and discovered the resurrection. It's a resurrection in the loving grace of Jesus. Before he was the Risen One, Jesus was the Suffering One who wept for his friend Lazarus, and who then met his own agony on the cross.

Mark Joseph Williams
Feast of St. Luke

The Last Drink

~

It is beautiful to see God's grace working in people. The most beautiful thing about it is to see how the desires of the soul, inspired by God, so fit in and harmonize with grace that holy things seem natural to the soul, seem to be part of its very self. That is what God wants to create in us—that marvelous spontaneity in which his life becomes perfectly ours and our life his, and it seems inborn in us to act as his children, and to have his light shining out of our eyes.

—Thomas Merton

When I left the business dinner with colleagues, stumbled into my Mini Cooper, and pulled out onto the highway a few hours shy of midnight, I knew what would come next. Instead of heading home to my sleeping wife and our four young children tucked in by her, not me, I sloppily steered the car as though on automatic pilot to yet another place to have one more drink—like so many times before.

My life had become unmanageable. And before I would embrace the first step in Alcoholics Anonymous—acknowledge that I was powerless over alcohol—I would have to experience what so many others did, before that first step: bottoming out. For now, I had no idea what "being in the rooms" meant. Before I would reckon with humility, I would meet humiliation.

I steered my way to the seediest bar to be alone in my cups to cap off the night. One more shot, that's all. Bed could wait. My wife could wait. My kids could wait.

Alone, in a sea of people I had never met nor would ever see again, I found a place behind the long circular bar. It was a dark cubicle with one large black leather chair, one small black plastic table, and three walls covered with black shag carpet. The floor beneath the chair, the table, and the makeshift walls had the same rough black rug. Already drunk, I fell into the chair.

I ordered a nightcap from the lap dancer, who crawled toward me on her knees while she touched her breasts, which were round and beautiful, resting behind a red see-through strapless bra. I felt aroused as she neared. Over her head, I could see another dancer in the middle of the bar, wrapped around a thin silver pole. Her skin was as pale as a pinewood derby model car, and she wore her flowing brunette hair up, so I had no other choice but to look right at the tattoo—an eagle—covering her back, which spread from the crack of her ass just above her pink panty to the base of her neck.

The small plastic table was full of empty and half-filled glasses. I had two dancers on top of me. The black leather chair held the three of us. I could hear some song from Madonna from the speakers above us. I kept staring at the black shag carpet on the wall nearest to my eyes, and I felt like I was touching the rug with my entire body.

Now the cubicle felt like a cave, and I was in a fetal position with the two lap dancers making out on top of me. I started to shake. It was dark as midnight. I was alone. I felt lost. Everything began to blur. I felt people staring at me, everyone in that bar, as my eyes rolled back in my head. My face touched the black carpet under me. My sweat mixed with the vomit—a pool in which I was now bathing.

How could this be? How could I, the respected husband, father, and corporate executive, be here—doing this?

I have no recollection of getting into my car. Nor do I remember driving into town. Now the lights—the red ones I had avoided so many times—got me.

The cuffs were tight, and as I pulled back, I felt them get even tighter. They broke the skin on my left wrist; blood, as red as the stripes of a new American flag at the Memorial Day parades of my youth, covered the French cuff sitting just above the fabric of the pinstriped suit sleeve. There were so many lights. Floodlights everywhere. Ten cops, maybe twenty.

The curtain opened on the stage, and I was there on a familiar street, cuffed, sweaty, bleeding, bloated, flushed, in front of good men and women doing their job, taking a drunk off the road, out of a car I had no business being in, away from a bar where just minutes before I was hiding, alone and isolating again like countless times before.

It took three cops to restrain me. They held me down before stuffing me into a squad car. As I continued to resist, they pushed me all the harder until I calmed down. I could see their fellow officers through the backseat window to my left; they circled the car like a group of deer hunters after bagging a prized buck. I was bagged and now facing the music. They had guns, handcuffs, badges, numerous SUVs, cameras, videotape recorders, in-board computers, pens, pads, uniforms, billy clubs, and German shepherds. They were sober; I was not. It was their street, not mine. I was scared and shook even harder, differently from earlier at the strip club. A fear I had never experienced before paralyzed me. I was trapped, spent, caught, broken. And so alone.

My fall from grace had arrived.

The anxiety was fierce, painful, crippling. After being locked up for a few hours, the cop in the station took my driver's license and drove me home. Karen, my bride, my wife, the one who always stuck by me and loved me deeply, was awakened by the knock on the door at 4 a.m. Before her she saw her husband, lover, friend, and a broken man—lost, distant, quiet, and defeated. Yet again I had let her down.

Once we were in the house, the officer pulled away. Maybe Karen hoped that this was truly the time, the moment I would finally surrender and stop drinking. Her embrace was gentle, touching. But sleep wouldn't come for days. And any kind of comfort would take much, much longer.

~

"There is the type of man who is unwilling to admit that he cannot take a drink. He plans various ways of drinking. He changes his brand of his environment," wrote William D. Silkworth, the psychiatrist who treated Bill Wilson, co-founder of AA, in the "The Doctor's Opinion" within the 1939 volume of Alcoholics Anonymous *Big Book.*

There is the type who always believes that after being entirely free from alcohol for a period of time he can take a drink without danger. There is the manic-depressive type, who is, perhaps the least understood by his friends, and about whom a whole chapter could be written. Then there are types entirely normal in every respect except in the effect alcohol has upon them. They are often able, intelligent, friendly people. All these, and many others, have one symptom in common: they cannot start drinking without developing the phenomenon of craving. This phenomenon . . . sets them apart as a distant entity. It has never been, by any treatment with which we are familiar, permanently eradicated. The only relief we have to suggest is entire abstinence.

I had no clue where abstinence would lead. But that night I discovered the bottoming out that would precipitate a profound change to my life.

2

Tour of Duty

~

Let us then with confidence draw near to the throne of grace, that we may receive mercy and find grace to help in time of need.

—Hebrews 4:16

On December 9, 1968, as my father lay dying, I had pulled a stool next to him in his room at Mount Sinai Hospital in New York City. A nuclear veteran—the common term for military personnel who work with or around nuclear weapons—at age forty he had acute leukemia and he lay in a full protective bubble. To touch him I had to use a rubber glove that extended from a plastic sleeve. He turned his head toward me and fought a smile as his hollowed eyes reached mine.

At the time, I was an altar boy in the Catholic Church, and I felt like I was among the women at the foot of the cross. Looking upward, I witnessed someone I loved with all my heart dying before me, yet I could not feel his flesh against mine. I had no idea what caused his cancer, why he was in this contained Calvary. Did he die, like Christ, to save others somehow in his own small way here on earth? Why was he taken so young? Was my father a sacrificial lamb for a greater cause? His loss opened this door of questions but closed for me many more as the grief set in.

Two hours later my father died. I had just turned twelve, and even as I faced a raw grief, I didn't realize that my darkest days were ahead. His death left our family shattered. My mother fell prey to her alcoholism, and I fell prey to her escalating physical and mental abuse and to the emotional and sexual abuse of some male members of the community.

No story of being a victim of sexual abuse is without a backstory, sometimes several backstories. Mine is the story of a child made vulnerable by circumstance, unmoored by circumstance. Knowing of my loss and our grief, father figures from the community sought me out. Some were well-intentioned, bringing support. Others were not, bringing shame and confusion. How was I, a young boy, to discern the intentions of the few who harmfully strayed, preying on a fatherless child desperately looking for a father?

My story also begins in a sense, sixteen years earlier, with my father's story when during his Korean War tour of duty, he was stationed in the Nevada Desert. Whisked away in the middle of the night by his commanding superiors with soldiers like him who learned the ropes at boot camp in San Luis Obispo in the foothills of California, he fully expected to head across the Pacific to Korea but ended up in the next state east.

My father's Ground Zero was smack in the middle of a desert on US soil. Regardless of the circumstance and the experiment my father and his fellow Army men inherited, these young soldiers, I've come to believe, embraced their defense of freedom by honoring our country and doing "what was needed" to battle the infiltration of Communism in the world. It took me thirty years to begin to fathom that my father actually believed this; in fact, a retired four-star army general remarked to me once while I was in my corporate years, "Your father was a patriot," With an absolute clarion voice.

Such ambition, a badge of honor, a complicated and crushing fate. Nevada was where the nuclear testing took place. My father told no one where he was. My mother, to whom he was engaged at the time, could not send letters there; she sent them to California, where they remained, unread. For about a year, my father stayed close to these sites. Death traps. The Pentagon believed that blowing up atomic bombs in contained surroundings would provide greater insight to our government's hired physicists and other creators of these doomsday missiles, to better understand how these devices could be more strategically used in war.

Unfathomable lethal weaponry. There was no turning back. Setting off nuclear bombs in front of innocent soldiers would demonstrate superiority on the world's military battlefield, even as the government knew that the soldiers there, like my father, were human guinea pigs.

Hiroshima and Nagasaki were destroyed less than a decade before, as World War II came to a close and the Japanese finally surrendered to the United States aboard a ship in the Pacific theater for history to record. History also included my father as an actor on this atomic stage.

Another part of the backstory of what made someone like me vulnerable to those who played the father figure was also the history of domestic violence in my family. Domestic violence existed long ago, but families almost never got caught and rarely were charged with any crime. In my immediate family it was commonplace—as was the confusing complexity of sometimes loving care with interludes of violence. I recall incidents where my father would throw my mother against his Volkswagen Bug again and again as they physically fought each other in our garage.

It was that same Bug that eight months before my father passed away, I drove with him, admiring how he downshifted and pumped the clutch with the ease of Mario Andretti at Indianapolis. I had looked forward to sitting next to my father and watching him drive to his weekly match with his friend, Hank. It was our special time together, and then the addition of Hank's presence.

It was Saturday, April 6, 1968, just two days after Martin Luther King Jr. had been killed in Memphis by James Earl Ray. About halfway to our destination, I asked my father why Dr. King was murdered. My father, keeping his eyes on the road, spoke softly, "People with a different color skin than ours are sometimes not liked, even hated, and that's why he was killed. Son, as long as you live, you must never think this way, you must accept all people, whatever color they are and love all."

At the game, as I looked on, my father and Hank hit the ball as hard as they could, ran to the net, and retreated to the baseline as fast as they could.

My dad and Hank loved to compete. Every game seemed to last longer than the one before. They were sweating like a kid facing a first pulled tooth. I was mesmerized by their intensity. They were good.

For about two hours now I'd been watching my father and Hank play tennis. My father hit a slicing backhand shot that curved away from Hank's outstretched left arm. The ball caught the back tape, giving my father the point. I sensed the bursting of energy around me. I could see the faint yellow of forsythia bushes behind the court's fencing ready to come alive. Seagulls yacking by the ocean, just over the nearby dunes, were as loud as the siren from our fire station signaling 5 p.m. every night.

My father crossed the court to the left, making his way just behind the backcourt stripe where he would continue the game holding serve, having just gone up 40–15 on Hank. Before he tossed the ball above him to pound his serve, my father fell hard to the pavement. He just lay there, motionless. I stood up and watched, staying where I was, scared. Hank bolted toward my father, jumped the net, and got to him. Someone must have seen what happened and called 911. Smartphones wouldn't arrive for decades. In the park there were pay phones. Soon police and an ambulance arrived.

The ionizing radiation that had pierced my father as he witnessed twenty-six nuclear tests in the Nevada desert so long ago had taken hold. Only once in the following eight months did he come home from the hospital. He turned forty in the hospital. I turned twelve while he was in the hospital. In the middle of that eighth month, he died on a Monday evening, no longer able to fight the acute leukemia that raised its ugly head on that tennis court.

It was as if a bomb had gone off inside him like the bombs he had seen during his tour. This was the same man who'd taken a belt to me and slapped my sister. This was my father who'd drunk more than I ever knew, because he wasn't around long enough and probably, like me, was good at hiding his drink and even better at isolating himself. And this was a man who beat my mother at times and at other times loved her exuberantly.

I tried to bury the demons that marked my father's life. His violence was overshadowed a good part of the time by his charm and a manner I liked even though I hardly knew him. Dad died early. His cancer tore him apart. And his behavior tore all of us, my family, apart.

My mother was violent, too, and she fought her own demons until her death from breast cancer. Her behavior, like my father's, also tore us apart, the family now left behind: my sister and me. What was in their backgrounds that made them fight, claw, and rip each other to shreds time and time again? I don't know. I still wonder.

Their screams chased me into a den of fear. Christmastime 1961. I was five. I walked timidly across the parquet floor from my bedroom into the narrow hallway facing my parents' bedroom. I was shaking uncontrollably, like a frozen stray during winter's worst, witnessing my father throw my mother across their bed, as she hit the back of her head against the large mirror that covered half of one wall from ceiling to floor. I ran back to my room, still shaking, terrified. Their screams never seemed to end.

Several years later, on a summer night in late June when the light stays radiant enough to see colors expose shades of surprise, I watched as my father threw my mother against the car—the Volkswagen Bug. The air, warm and insipid, like a stream of hot steam penetrated the open garage. My mother always fought back and came at him kicking, her legs reaching his waist. Some kicks actually landed in his gut, pushing my father back across the cold cement floor leading out to our driveway.

Down the street is where I would play stickball with my friends when they did come around. And from there I saw and heard. The yelling paused after my father died. But just for a moment. The demons always lurked in my mother's core and would strike again and again and again. Like the time she broke a wooden clothes hanger over my wife's head and the cops came. Or another time when she appeared unannounced three hours from her house at our first-floor apartment, our initial home as a married couple, demanding to see our just-born first child who was not there. Before she sped off, she threw an end table through the front picture window. Glass in a thousand little pieces. A woman, a mother, a widow, a grandmother, a mother-in-law, a sister, all shattered. All the broken pieces of her life matched the sun-soaked and blinding shattered glass that covered the floor of our porch.

Curiously, remarkably, and astonishingly, despite the staggering chaos between them, my parents maintained a capacity to love. Between the violent episodes I found my own measure of peace—but I remained haunted for years by how they hurt each other, in their short time with me on earth.

They were alcoholics of the violent kind and never had the

opportunity nor appeared, from my own experience of them, to have made the searching and moral inventory of themselves, as Catholics and their tradition invited. As people whom I believe loved God, and were loved by God, they like so many others of their generation didn't discover the tools, the step of that moral inventory, so necessary in recovery to obtain interior freedom and peace of mind, body, and soul.

I have held onto hope through my own asking of God for peace to enter my inner soul that their Pentecost away from the world, beyond their earthen trek, could be imagined as a journey of forgiveness, and I trusted God surely had listened to them, removed the defects, sadness, and madness that formed most of the days of their lives. I know they were broken, but a piercing redemption has touched me deeply as my life continued both drunk and sober, and I continue to feel their presence, like the sun that rises each day.

I yearn to know that prayer still reaches them and me. "So what do we pray for?" James Martin, SJ, asked in his book *Learning to Pray: A Guide for Everyone*:

> To my mind we can pray for anything good that we might need. Let's remember that one reason we pray is because we need to. How could we not ask for help in the face of life's misfortunes? We imagine ourselves standing before God, we become acutely aware of our limitations. Approaching God, the source of all good things, we come face-to-face with our unmet needs. Overall, in the divine presence we experience the human condition, which is finite, limited, needful. The obvious and appropriate response is to pray for what we need.

In those early years, God must have been speaking to me too, but I didn't realize it.

However dark my fear was, I was held close by God, because I've lived to tell my story—or as it is called in AA, I've been able to give my "qualification," an offering that has brought me home to the Church, a Church that hurt me—a Church that also has redeemed me. It took time for the teaching of truth, that torrent of grace, to reach me and free me from the paralyzing grasp within. But God heard my often unspoken but grief-stricken prayers.

At his funeral, the American flag draped my father's coffin as his best friend, Mel—Jewish, and married to Eileen, a Roman Catholic—spoke to the congregation before the concluding rite at the funeral Mass. "Joe was a classy guy," he said. "He was and still is my best friend." I still remember the eloquence of that moment.

I still think about my father each day. I remember him dying. I hold his advice in me. I recall fondly how he loved to dress sharp. I remember him playing catch with me. But what I remember most is his rage. I remember his drinking, but not as much as my mother's.

It is said in recovery *identify*, but do not compare. The fact is, they both drank excessively, which led to turmoil. Like most families, we struggled with life's challenges, and alcohol more often than not fueled dysfunction. When I think about my father, I wonder about the demons inside that must have consumed him. I wonder about my mother's demons as well and what she may have gone through as a young girl.

Maybe my father's demons were born in that Nevada desert. Maybe elsewhere. Something led him to drink. He drank. He became violent. And he was also the same man who told me, "Love all."

As a nuclear veteran, my father may not have realized the enormity of what he was witnessing and how the entire world could be gone in an instant with the proliferation of nuclear weaponry in the hands of governments across the planet. Was this a weight too heavy to carry on his shoulders and in his heart? In the aftermath of witnessing acts of war contrary to the preservation of human life many solders resort to violence. Some who kill live with this profound wound of taking another life, more so when a victim is a bystander, an innocent. Was this moral injury my father lived with? Did he ultimately not feel a connection to this world after his nuclear tour, bearing a pain too painful to bear?

When we suffer moral distress, we typically get lost in convictions about our badness, our unforgivable failures as human beings. What's harder to grasp—but vital for sufferers to take in—is that moral distress actually springs from our essential goodness, which is bound up in our caring relationships. When we find ourselves in situations that disrupt natural human connection—when we're pressured to cause others harm and do nothing—we plunge into a form of radical distress. In these crises, we're faced with a kind of Sophie's Choice, wherein we have to make the excruciating decision to either protect others or protect ourselves, in some cases with life-or-death consequences.

> When we choose ourselves, often under duress, the ethical part of us suffers. And our souls drop into darkness. That darkness may lead to depression and thoughts of ending one's life, or it may trigger a kind of self-protection freezing of the spirit, a sense that one is unworthy of being loved which then leads to the abandonment of care and compassion for others. The heart of moral repair involves guiding the soul out of its dark place and into the light again. This is hard and harrowing work: for some people, it takes years to heal their splintered spirits and recover wholeness. Others never do. But the invitation for therapists (healers, those accompanying victims / survivors) is clear: we need to help morally distressed people experience their essential

goodness, which includes a process of breaking through isolation and sharing their experience, feeling fully heard and acknowledged, and finally, witnessing others share responsibility for the larger social ills that have contributed to their moral distress.

We need to approach moral pain not as part of mental disorder, but rather an injury of the soul.

—Jack Saul, in *Psychotherapy Networker*,
September / October 2023

My father never spoke about his moral injury. He never told a soul. His own soul remained damaged till death. And his was a damage that I, in part, carried too. One story alongside another.

Moral injury affects so many, who respond to the pain in varied ways—violence, drinking, an inability to sustain loving care. Years later I met another man suffering piercing moral injury. He was one of my clinical forensic clients, Lawrence. Having served in Afghanistan, he returned home traumatized from assignments that included the photographing of hundreds of civilians and fellow soldiers strewn dead across a Kabul hillside after a suicide bombing in order to provide his commanding officers details so they could assess "operational missteps." The hole in the soul Lawrence came back with contributed to his deep psychological dysfunction. Sadly and tragically, he wound up killing an African American homeless man on a NYC street with a dagger. War clouded this man's previous acceptance of all people regardless of ethnicity and color of skin.

When I interviewed him in solitary at Rikers Correctional Facility, he showed little remorse and showed me what a top military man described to me as the *1,000-mile stare* that so many veterans display in response to the horror they saw, felt, carried inside. After four hours of building trust with me behind the glass of his cell, the stare became something else as he teared up and shared something he'd never before told anyone: as a nine-year-old, he had been sexually abused by a teacher who was tutoring him in an after-school program. I listened in silence, astonished. What I had been through had happened to this young man now serving life behind bars. He also witnessed what my father had so many years before: the inexplicable misery of war regardless of what side you were on.

Moral injury doesn't choose a side, there is no discriminating factor; the raw pain and unimaginable hurt is universal. What Lawrence did in killing an innocent man was absolutely wrong and absent any justification whatsoever. But as I listened, I also heard how his past abuse also played a part in what happened later in his life. Pain begets pain. Besides everything else he endured psychologically, my client, Lawrence, was never free of the stranglehold his early sexual trauma had on him. As the defense attorney who brought me on as an expert psychological mitigation specialist said to me before I first met Lawrence, *"Mark, there is something there, he is a lost soul."*

Like Lawrence and countless others around the globe, the backstory of being a vulnerable child affected the story of his later life. This is the kind of youngster the World Health Organization would have included in their statistics about children sexually abused, regardless of the year along the human journey. Among the statistics are these:

- One in five women, and one in thirteen men report experiencing sexual abuse before their eighteenth birthday. Because of the shame, stigma, and fear associated with their experience, at least 60 percent of child sexual abuse victims never disclose their abuse.
- Children living in homes marked by parental discord, divorce, or domestic violence have a higher risk of being sexually abused.

- According to a 2003 National Institute of Justice report, three out of four adolescents who have been sexually assaulted were victimized by someone they knew well.

And today, the Catholic Church continues to wrestle with the sins of abuse within its own institution, where the vulnerable are not healed, but further harmed. And yet, it has been the vulnerable who have spoken out:

As Pope Francis wrote in *Let Us Dream*:

> The culture of abuse, whether sexual, or of power and conscience, began to be dismantled first by victims and their families, who in spite of their pain, were able to carry through their struggle for justice and help alert and heal society of this perversity. As I will not tire of saying with sorrow and shame, these abuses were also committed by some members of the Church. In these past years we have taken important steps to stamp out abuses and to engender a culture of care able to respond swiftly to accusations. Creating the culture will take time, but it is an unavoidable commitment which must be no more abuse—whether sexual, or of power and conscience—either inside or outside the Church. In the Church, this sense of entitlement is the cancer of clericalism, as I call it, that perversion of the vocation to which priests are called.

Every day I think about my father, now a little over a half-century removed from his death, I often wonder how God held me in that dark hour and the darker hours that followed his death, the beginning of the sexual abuse.

Now, I realize that I had my own moral injury. Somehow in and through the "soul pain" and truly also the psychological pain, for some reason I cannot explain, I never resorted to anger, to turning away from the Church. Maybe early on I understood the Eucharist, the cross was with me and held me. Maybe God was leading me through the suffering of the cross, to be present for others.

In the rooms of recovery you often hear that God doesn't give us more than we can handle. Maybe in time Christ would indeed redeem me. But back then, I had no idea how to put words or feelings to what I had gone through so young.

As the drink took me over too, any interior injury would be numbed by the addiction that started to take hold. In the deep recesses of my core, death and abuse took a seat. Even as something was at work, unseen, in those devastating years, in my time of need: *grace.*

~

Soon after the death of my father, I fell victim to predatory behavior by two men in my community, one of them a priest. In the intervening decades, I numbed the pain through alcoholism and denial. And it would be years until I eventually would find true spiritual mentors, sponsors, and doctors to help me heal. There was no direct route. It was a long journey, but somehow doors opened one by one, as I understood my own story, as I listened to the stories of others abused by priests within the Church. I found a desire to advocate for other abuse victims.

In 2019 I learned about a still-forming survivor-led organization committed to healing vulnerable children who have faced sexual violation and was invited to serve as a co-founder of the Global Collaborative. Under the remarkable leadership of Global Collaborative co-founder Dr. Jennifer Wortham with the support of Michael Hoffman and Fatima Maada Bio, the United Nations in 2022—galvanized by our efforts—established in perpetuity November 18 as the World Day for the Prevention of and

Healing from Child Sexual Exploitation, Abuse, and Violence. And for many involved—especially those like me harmed by Catholic clergy—it was especially moving and necessary for those seeking change and accountability in the Catholic Church—to also witness the participation of the Holy See's Archbishop Gabriele Caccia, in his role as Permanent Observer to the United Nations.

3

The First Drink

When I was a child, I used to talk as a child, reason as a child, think as a child; when I became a man, I put aside childish things. At present we see indistinctly, as in a mirror, but then face to face. At present, I know partially; then I shall know fully, as I am fully known. So faith, hope, love remain, these three; but the greatest of these is love.

—1 Corinthians 13:11–13

St. Paul's well-known teaching on love in the First Letter to the Corinthians, chapter 13, comes down to this: saying we love without acting in love is worthless. Everything we do must be done with love.

Yet on and on hearts are broken often by those whose motivation isn't love. Children in our midst who yearn to grow, discover, and embrace the early fruits of life should never be stripped of love, subjected to another's self-possession and the void of love masking as so many other things. It's crushing to face what no one should face. It is a living hell with seemingly no exit. I know.

East Hampton, on the South Fork at the tip of Long Island,

is a place embraced by sands that roll calmly to an ocean calling out the gull's song, to a sea bluer than a pea jacket, to salt
as fresh as summer primrose. A sensual place, it is at the same
time a holy ground where the spirit lives. And it is the setting
of creation where my life began, emotionally ended, and began
again anew. East Hampton is where my innocence was lost,
where I was raped when I was thirteen.

Some six months after my father died, a public school teacher
at the elementary school, a devout Catholic, began to come often
to our house. I wasn't sure why. I don't recall how he and my
mother, a decade older than he, met. Close to thirty, still living at home with his parents, he liked to drink, and he and my
mother would down scotch after scotch in front of me and my
younger sister. He dressed in strong shades of red, yellow, blue,
and green, and favored corduroy pants and cable knit sweaters.
He was chunky. His face was round as a beach ball and coupled
with his wire-rimmed glasses, he reminded me of Captain Kan-
garoo, the main character of a popular kids' television show. As
he smoked and drank with my mother, he would stare at me a
lot. There was nowhere else for me to go, so I usually was around
when he came over to drink, smoke, talk, and laugh with my
mother. And stare at me.

I recall hearing conversation between them that was superfi-
cial: types of scotch, fashion, restaurants in town, celebrity folk
who frequented places my mother worked nights as a waitress.
Nothing more than that.

He exuded a type of confidence like someone in charge. His
staring at me was creepy and controlling. And weirded me out.
I remember him telling my mother that I was good looking
and that he liked my long, flowing brown hair. He had a Ford
Thunderbird with a hood that looked as long as a football field as
he drove away from our house. He could down three scotches in

an hour and another before he left, usually no more than a half hour later. Before leaving, he would always put his arm around my shoulder and say he would see me soon; then he would wink at my mother and wish her a good night.

Around the first anniversary of my father's passing, this teacher arranged to pick me up for the afternoon, saying he would "take care of me" for the afternoon. It was close to Christmas. He knew exactly what he was doing, what he was setting up. We wound up at his house, early evening. No one was home. After he got me drunk, he raped me. That was my first drink. When I flash back to that night, often, I recall it as an endless dark taking hold, the sense of losing hope.

The teacher and I were in his parents' bedroom and their bed. Shaking, I was forced to do things I had never done. Oral. Anal. It was painful. It was raw. I was naked. Scared. Drunk. I lived a world of pain at thirteen.

I felt slaughtered, broken, lonely. I didn't know where I was or how anxiety had taken such a hold on me. I couldn't stop moving even as I was crying inside. But I wondered, where are my tears? I am afraid and alone, and cannot cry.

I was silent. And I prayed deeply, crying for God to help in my aloneness.

That was the night my drinking started, in that kitchen. I was hooked by alcohol, believing its false promise of self-medication, of numbing. I became obsessed with its taste, its power over me. I had the gene. There was alcohol in my bloodline. That night, my innocence died and left me with no choice but to drink again and again and again. The disease of alcoholism further metastasized beyond my genetic disposition. My destined future, my sexually violated past took root, drunk. As it says in the First Step of AA's *Twelve Steps and Twelve Traditions*—often referred to as the 12 and 12:

Under the lash of alcoholism, we are driven to AA, and there we discover the fatal nature of our situation. Then, and only then, do we become as open-minded to conviction and as willing to listen as the dying can be. We stand ready to do anything which will lift the merciless obsession from us.

I often reflect on that dark, confusing night of my first drink. The stage was set for me to be raped, to be pierced. Booze and grooming—perfect together. I was so young, so vulnerable. My first drink would be the first of many. Every day for thirty-five years after that night, I drank. And drank.

According to the Franciscan Richard Rohr in his book *On the Threshold of Transformation: Daily Meditations for Men*, "The spiritual life is a great recycler; nothing really goes away. Everything that has happened to us remains, and not healed, will just keep showing itself in newly disguised forms." Later he quotes the words of poet Robert Bly from a January 1990 interview with Bill Moyers: "You don't get rid of demons, you just educate them."

Buried in such tangible confusion, the pain of that night was just too much to bear. The shame cut my core.

I'd heard people say that God does not give us more than we can handle. But at so many times in my young life and my adult life, I wasn't so sure.

The only way for me to begin to comprehend the unfathomable pain of that childhood night was to write about it. No other form went as deep as I needed as poetry. Not long ago I picked up a pen and wrote:

Innocence Lost

*A mere child, young and broken by the death of Dad a
  year before.*

*I was lonely, trying to cope, fragile; seeking God, wanting
    more.
He, the teacher, brought me there, to his house to see
    what, I wasn't sure,
But it seemed fine, a mere child, accepting his tour.*

*Candles burning, thick red, green, white like those of
    Christmastime.
In that setting silence only broken by a clock's chime.
I tasted the scotch; drank more and more,
The trace of peat taking over, reaching my core.
Alcohol grasping the moment, taking hold,
Changing me, truth be told.*

*Now it was his turn to grasp and take
What was not his—me—like a piece of cake.
His right hand found my knee; his lips were curled, long
    and pink.
Drunk now, unable to flee, no strength, only to sink.*

*I caved in doing what he sought.
A mere child, I had been caught.
Pants dropped with him behind,
Feeling the sharp penetration of the worst kind.*

*Like a marlin's escape from a fishhook at sea,
I screamed for him to set me free.*

*His scream of pleasure, my scream of despair.
Shattered and threadbare. Shaken, scared, trembling,
    alone.*

A mere child, God's voice a distant drone.

4

Clerical Silence

*Christian spirituality does not apologize for the fact that,
within it, the most central of all mysteries is the paschal
one, the mystery of suffering, death, and transformation.
In Christian spirituality, Christ is central and central
to Christ is his death and rising to new life so as to send
us a new Spirit.*

—Ronald Rolheiser

On the last Sunday of February 1972 our priest invited me to
drive with him to Cathedral College in Douglaston, Queens,
from East Hampton, Long Island, some ninety miles to the
west. He invited me to attend a special Mass with him that late
afternoon for new seminarians committing their lives to the
ordained priesthood. My mother approved. I went with him to
this liturgy and afterward would have dinner at the home of his
older brother and sister-in-law who lived about halfway between
my home and our destination.

The pastor drove up our driveway about noontime. It was an
unseasonably warm day, even though snow still blanketed our
yard. It was his sixty-first birthday; I was fifteen.

Following the Mass, we drove back east to his family's house.

Before we reached the main property, my pastor said that he wanted to show me a favorite spot nearby, a cove where native ospreys frequented. With our windows opened a pinch, the cove smelled of salt, embraced by a meadow of flowing yellow grass—tall, lush, gentle, whispering—as his French sedan rested, parked now in the silent beauty around us. Seats side by side, tilted like cots, ready for sleep. No one around. Only him and me.

The pastor removed his Roman collar, unbuttoned his shirt, and stopped when he reached his belt buckle. He then asked me to unbuckle my belt and unzip my pants, and as soon as I had done both, he put his right hand down, between my skin and my underwear, found my penis, held it, stroked it, and said softly, as he closed his eyes, "Thank you, thank you, thank you." The pastor then asked me to return the favor to him, unbuckle his belt, unzip his trousers, and touch him in the same way he had touched me. After I had done so, he again offered softly, eyes closed, "Thank you, thank you, thank you."

The setting sun enveloped us as we drove back toward the main country road to his brother's house—a white clapboard structure, topped with a cedar wood shingled roof, like those along the ocean where my father took me to fly my first kite when I was four years old—for his birthday celebration.

I responded to the pain with a silence that brought comfort but concealed everything. What was going on in my mind during the years I was abused was silence? The pain, the truth, the shame: all lay dormant in the bowels of my silent being, in the depths of my soul. I'm not sure how all that happened to me stayed buried—the violations and all that went into being groomed, forced, cornered, cajoled, bought, and stroked—how it all could stay so quiet, pushed even deeper down in the core of my being.

Life just went on. Drinking, certainly, was a two-edged sword.

Drink numbed me, kept me from dealing with the pain and the dark shame. It was too scary; it would unglue me. I wasn't even sure what I might have been hiding. I simply worked diligently, drank constantly, to forget the past, or rather bury the demons, keep them at bay.

Fear consumed me. I lived, like so many, in the stranglehold of loneliness, unable to find solitude, to listen for God's love. I just couldn't understand in those early years what exactly I had gone through. Ongoing shame led me to blame myself. I acted out. I lied. I cheated. I avoided. I stole. I ran. I wandered. I left. I cried. I drank. I continued to drink.

As it is often said in recovery, "Time takes time." I know now the clues that God always loved me were present, waited for me to see his love. How we love, how we are to love. The first letter of John's Gospel teaches (4:19): We love because God first loved us.

My two abusers, on the face of it, seemed to act with kindness, showering me with gifts. But I felt trapped, strangely obliged to stay in the relationships. As an adolescent is developing psychologically, emotionally, physically, sexually, and then is hit with trauma—especially sexual violation—the effects can last well into adulthood.

~

In my current forensic work, I come across horrific stories of sexual trauma. And one way I assess a client's history around sexual exploitation, violence, or abuse is to ask a question from the Adverse Childhood Experience (ACE) Questionnaire supported by the CDC and Kaiser Permanente for a study measuring the impact of childhood trauma into adulthood: *While you were growing up, during the first 18 years of your life, did an adult or person at least 5 years older than you ever touch or fondle you or have you touch their body in a sexual way, or attempt or actually have oral, anal, or vaginal intercourse with you?*

> *Now, in my life when I have the opportunity to speak and meet fellow alcoholics in the rooms of AA in whatever town I'm speaking, I recall the marvelous section of the Twelfth Step of AA that I recite as I bask in being lifted by a Higher Power I know as Jesus Christ.*
>
> *Practically every AA member declares that no satisfaction has been deeper and no joy greater than in a Twelfth Step job well done. To watch the eyes of men and women open with wonder as they move from darkness into light, to see their lives quickly fill with new purpose and meaning, to see whole families reassembled, to see the alcoholic received back into his [/her] community in full citizenship, and above all to watch these people awaken to the presence of a loving God in their lives—these things are the substance of what we receive as we carry AA's message to the next alcoholic.*

This question, once I am able to build trust with a client, amazingly hits the mark, and often a defendant who must go before a judge for sentencing brings a greater understanding from discovering how a current response to past events later in life plays out in clear psychological dysfunction, even criminal behavior.

Because of what I have been through with my own abuse, I often feel that God has called me to do this work, ask these questions, and identify with those I come across in the criminal justice system as part of an assigned defense team. When more often than not a sentence is reduced by a person's simply telling the *story* of their sexual trauma history, I am humbled that my mitigation support opens a window into the reasons people act out of their own pain and histories.

For a very long time I did not tell my own story. In fact, I didn't tell a soul about my abuse; I did not even know its name, that it was abuse. I just went along with it and lived its pain. Becoming a daily drinker at such a young age allowed me to shield from the realities of it all. The irony of it was that the drinking allowed me to avoid what was really going on. The drink helps. Until it stops helping. Often, you'll hear people say that in the rooms of recovery.

My introduction to drinking alcoholically was complex, and I would say even mysterious in that, during this whole time I somehow remained close to God, to a faith that was maturing. And close to the Church. I am not sure why this was so but even in, the depths of what I was going through, I maintained a fairly normal life for an adolescent, whatever normal meant.

I suppose from the perspective of others around me in school and the community where I grew up, I must have seemed like there could not possibly be anything happening to me to give anyone pause or any inclination to investigate, ask questions, dive in, and explore just what might be going on behind closed doors.

Among the many AA slogans that hit home with their seemingly simple message yet profound significance about the human road is one that has stuck with me over the years: "We are as sick as our secrets." This was true for me until so many years later when the secrets demanded their own release from bondage, pushing me toward freedom from my own self-bondage, from a crippling self-centered belief that the world revolves around me, as it does for any transparent addicted person who, having displayed the courage to come clean, finally admits self-defeat. And in that, discovers a willingness to be self-forgetting, to realize that others and God—a Higher Power—reign higher than oneself. In service to others, in loving God, this far outweighs any self-gratification. This is the path of humility that the Seventh Step of the 12 and 12 (*Twelve Steps and Twelve Traditions*) captures best:

Then, in AA, we looked and listened. Everywhere we saw failure and misery transformed by humility into priceless assets. We heard story after story of how humility had brought strength out of weakness. In every case, pain had been the price of admission into a new life. But this admission price had purchased more than we expected. It brought a measure of humility, which we soon discovered to be a healer *of pain. We began to fear pain less, and desire humility more than ever.*

Every story tells another story, contains multitudes of stories. The priest who molested me was a man of intellect coming from a life of privilege. A convert from a staunch Episcopal background, he was influenced by a message of peace he heard by a Catholic bishop in Munich close to the outbreak of World War II during his studies in Germany. He followed a road that led him to eventual conversion to Roman Catholicism and then to the ordained priesthood. Because of his fluency in German, he spent the war years in the navy intercepting code from German submarines to protect United States naval ships.

Six decades later, well after his death, and near the end of the worst period of the worldwide coronavirus pandemic, I had a meeting that I can only conclude was divinely arranged. I was introduced virtually to a woman religious, a Benedictine nun living in a monastic community in Germany. A priest from Paderborn served as our translator. This nun and I, approximately the same age, were spiritual companions for each other. She told me her story, only requesting I not use her full name to protect confidentiality. From the start I found this connection to Munich profound for both of us, with both of our abusers.

In part our conversation stemmed from a January 2022 report commissioned by the Archdiocese of Munich-Freising, regarding the sexual abuse crisis between 1945 and 2019. The report identified 497 victims of abuse, mainly young males, and concluded that retired Pope Benedict XVI failed to take action against clerics in four cases of alleged sexual abuse during his time as archbishop in this part of Germany from 1977 to 1982.

The pope emeritus was believed by many in the Church to be the first pope to resign as pontiff in some six hundred years due to the piercing stress he was enduring with the worldwide sexual abuse crisis in the Church. His resignation led to the election of the first pope in history from the Global South: Jorge Bergoglio, who took the name of Francis, another first in the annals of papal history. After this report came out, and as his ill health advanced, Benedict XVI appeared to have a change of heart regarding gaps in his understanding and protection of victims of abuse, something he appeared to miss as archbishop four decades prior, admitting he arguably could and should have acted differently.

With the assistance of aides, due to his advanced age, he wrote a letter two weeks after the report's release to the people of the Archdiocese of Munich-Freising, a portion of which is below:

In all my meetings, especially during my many Apostolic Journeys, with the victims of sexual abuse by priests, I have seen at firsthand the effects of a most grievous fault. And I have come to understand that we ourselves are drawn into this grievous fault whenever we neglect it or fail to confront it with the necessary decisiveness and responsibility, as too often happened and continues to happen. As in those meetings, once again I can only express to all victims of sexual abuse my profound shame, my deep sorrow and my heartfelt request for forgiveness. I have had great responsibilities in the Catholic Church. All the greater is my pain for the abuses and the errors that occurred in those different places during the time of my mandate. Each individual case of sexual abuse is appalling and irreparable. The victims of sexual abuse have my deepest sympathy and I feel great sorrow for each individual case.

Shortly after the confession of the retired pontiff, native son of Germany, my new friend and fellow survivor, whom I'll call "Sister B," wrote a letter to Benedict XVI, the former Cardinal Joseph Ratzinger when his alleged cover-up took place decades earlier in the Archdiocese of Munich-Freising, and received a confirmation of receipt from Archbishop Gänswein, Benedict's primary assistant. Translated, it reads, in part:

Esteemed Holy Father Pope Emeritus Benedict . . .

A few days ago you wrote a letter to the faithful of the Archdiocese of Munich-Freising which touched me deeply as a survivor of sexual abuse. Please allow me to thank you personally for it!

In due brevity the background: After a puerile vocation as a six-year-old girl I was searching for the right path when, at age 21, I fell into the hands of a Benedictine priest 35 years older than me. He committed violence on my body and soul and completely dominated me for 3 years until I entered the Abbey.

Since 2010, I have been more and more successful in recognizing the things that had occurred and I comprehend it no longer as my fault, as my own most grievous fault, but as what it really was and is: an abuse in all respects, even if it happened to me as a young adult woman.

Since then I have been trying to find a way to freedom under the word of the Lord: "The truth will set you free."

Regarding your letter of 6th February 2022: First of all, I would like to thank you for not avoiding an encounter with us, but that you have taken us into account, that you have held our gaze . . . , that you faced up to our suffering and thus gave us back some of our destroyed dignity. You expressed your pain and your compassion, and through your word of confession you took part of the responsibility for the crimes that have been committed in the Church, often "in the name of God." For this I thank you as a religious, a nun, who despite everything has been trying to seek God for 45 years now.

What has affected me personally most deeply, and what I desperately want you to know about: It was not possible for me until today—not after many conversations, confessions and trauma therapy—to forgive the criminal of my past, to forgive him his fault, for this reason: I attach forgiveness to the condition that the perpetrator recognized his fault, asking me for forgiveness. . . .

. . . Now, before you and in the presence of God, I want to forgive with all my heart and pardon my confrere for all that he has done to me and commend him to the mercy of God. I wish and pray that he has found a merciful judge beyond the dark door of death, a friend and brother, as you put it.

Why did it take a Pope's plea for forgiveness for me to touch my heart? Perhaps the wound was so deep, perhaps because I remained silent for so long, too long? . . .

As Sister B shared her letter with me and we spoke, I realized we both experienced a similar transformative benefit. Sister B and I bonded, encountered each other, cried together from different continents as we both stared into our respective computer screens. Grace was alive in us, in that very teary moment as details of place and connection to cardinals of the Church came together. As I relayed my story, I told her my priest abuser was a seminary classmate of another cardinal, Cardinal Joseph Bernardin, at Catholic University, a man I met in the summer of 1974 when he attended a biannual gathering for his 1952 class, that summer held at my parish in East Hampton. At that time, Bernardin, a man who years later would be falsely accused of sexually abusing a young seminary student soon before his death in 1996, was then archbishop of Cincinnati when I was asked to drive him from East Hampton to LaGuardia Airport after he was called back for a diocesan emergency.

During our nearly two-hour drive west to the airport, I remember him telling me that he was born the same year as my father, 1928, in response to my telling him the story of my father's death five years prior. I was taken by how sensitive and kind he was, expressing warmth about the loss I had gone through so young. Looking back, I have no idea if he had any suspicions about his classmate and friend, my priest and abuser.

Decades later, when I was in a better place emotionally in touch with my early trauma, I often wondered what the esteemed Cardinal Bernardin knew about clergy abuse and what he did to address it. At the time he served the Archdiocese of Chicago, becoming known as a bridge-builder in and out of the Church. Did he value the most vulnerable among us, God's children who suffered on the margins? Did he know his cleric friend crossed the line with me? And did he act toward justice?

As I spoke with Sister B, I also felt it providential that I had the opportunity to connect with the cardinal, as I followed Bernardin's ministry as a leader in the Church, notwithstanding someone accusing him of not acting (though I never did know) in regard to what I had gone through with his classmate.

Just thirteen days before his death in November 1996, his beautifully written short book *The Gift of Peace* was completed. In it Joseph Cardinal Bernardin wrote about his being falsely accused, the charges being dropped, and the reconciliation that followed with his accuser, a story that offered a thread of hope and both inspired and comforted me for many years.

Among the words I read in his book were these:

> But as I moved behind the brace of microphones, I felt that I was literally standing before the entire world, and yet I felt very much alone. The most important thing I had going for me at that moment was my forty-two years of ordained ministry, my name, and my reputation. But there was also an inner strength, and I am convinced that the Lord was giving me that strength. For me, this moment of public accusation and inquiry was also a moment of grace. A moment of pain, but a moment of grace because I felt the great love and support that many people were giving me. Above all, it was a moment of spiritual growth. I felt that I was entering a new phase of my spiritual journey because of the events of those few days.

After the case was dropped, Cardinal Bernardin met the man who accused him falsely, a man dying of AIDS, who had lived near Philadelphia and St. Charles Borromeo Seminary.

The book continued:

> I explained to him that the only reason for requesting the meeting was to bring closure to the traumatic events of last winter by personally letting him know that I harbored no ill feelings toward him. I told him I wanted to pray with him for his physical and spiritual well-being. He replied that he had decided to meet with me so he could apologize for the embarrassment and hurt he had caused. In other words, we both sought reconciliation.

After praying together with his false accuser, Cardinal Bernardin said Mass for him and his friend who accompanied him, concelebrated by two priests present for this historic encounter.

> I then took a hundred-year-old chalice out of my case; this is a gift from a man I don't even know. He asked me to use it to say Mass for you one day. "Please," the false accuser responded tearfully, "let's celebrate Mass now."

Never in my entire priesthood have I witnessed a more profound reconciliation. The words I am using to tell this story cannot begin to describe the power of God's grace at work that afternoon. It was a manifestation of God's love, forgiveness, and healing that I will never forget.

Within two years of their reconciliation, both Cardinal Bernardin and the man who falsely accused him died. As I meditate on their synodal exchange—listening to each other, seeking to understand the other—I can only be grateful for my own time with Cardinal Bernardin, realizing that peace for me came from the reconciliation I witnessed within the words of the book. I, too, also found an encounter of forgiveness although my accusation of abuse was not false. Mine was true, piercing, real, raw. And I shared this story with Sister B as we met on that call, both recognizing in the other's story something so desirous of freedom.

The pastor who abused me served in the navy during World War II with fellow naval man and friend Cardinal Avery Dulles, SJ. They studied together at Harvard, both converted to the Roman Catholic faith, and my pastor was Dulles's godfather as well as the homilist at his first Mass in Washington, DC, in 1956, the year of my birth.

Like my curiosity regarding what people like Cardinal Bernardin knew about the far-ranging clerical sexual abuse perpetrated by peers—and those they considered friends—I have also wondered if Cardinal Dulles knew or suspected anything untoward about his friend, fellow cleric, and the man who abused me.

I also met Cardinal Dulles a few times during his tenure teaching at Fordham University before his death in 2008. As I said to Sister B, I have always found these convergences a mystery and part of a complex story I don't really have words for. Sometimes life just happens, but having had conversations with these two cardinals of the Church who were also very close friends to my abuser priest is sufficient reason to pause, to question, and to wonder what was known or suspected and what—if anything—was done to attend to the harm done, to those victims like me, whose lives often fell into addiction, deep psychological pain, immersed in darkness.

The Church in these last years and months has been in a process of the Synod of Synodality, a journey to imagine a different Church at this hour in the twenty-first century, a time to listen to one another, the ordained, religious, and all lay men and women across the world. It is an extraordinary moment in the life of the Church to take stock toward true renewal in communion, participation, and mission. God's people are being called. The abused among us must be listened to. And if the Holy Spirit is the protagonist of this synod, as Pope Francis has stressed, as a guide for the Church to truly imagine a different Church, one that includes all brothers and sisters more fully, especially those on the margins, most notably the poor in treasure and spirit, and beyond any hesitation those hurt by sexual abuse in the Church, then this Spirit who guides the Church, the one who entered my life all those years ago with these intersections, connections to my abuser, these churchmen known for their pastoral intellect to advance the message of Christ here on earth during their lives must have had some reason to live in me. Who is this protagonist Spirit? For me it must ultimately be the Trinity: God the

Father, God the Son, God the Holy Spirit. But what do all these encounters I had years ago leading up to today mean?

I don't have the answers. But some solace comes from a slogan in AA: *More will be revealed.*

Imagine for a moment, Cardinal Dulles articulating those thoughts he penned four decades ago in his 1977 book, *The Resilient Church,* to those who gathered in Rome for the first session of Francis's Synod on Synodality in October 2023, as Dulles echoed a Vatican II desire to grow in love, despite division, culture, clericalism, tension, yearning to find greater meaning in walking together in Christ's love. Dulles wrote:

> For my part, I believe that it is important for the Church to have a hierarchy somewhat shielded from the pressure of public opinion, though not unaware of what the people are thinking. Bishops endowed with a common sense, a moderate competence in theology, and a real sensitivity to pastoral needs can inestimably help to mediate the painful conflicts in which the Church is presently involved. Bishops are rarely avant-garde reformers and for the most part, in my opinion, should not be. Time must be given for the Church as a whole to absorb the shock of Vatican II. Time will be needed, also, for the reformers to develop a strategy that is based not simply on the axioms of the Enlightenment but on the full resources of the biblical and Catholic tradition.

What Avery Dulles spoke about nearly a half-century ago mirrors the spiritual reflection offered by Fr. Timothy Radcliffe, OP, at the close of the first Synod session in Rome:

> Humanity's first vocation in Paradise was to be gardeners. Adam tended creation, sharing in speaking God's creative

words, naming the animals. In these eleven months, will we speak fertile, hope-filled words, or words that are destructive and cynical? Will our words nurture the crop or be poisonous? Shall we be gardeners of the future or trapped in old sterile conflicts? We each choose.

Cardinal Dulles may or may not have had knowledge that his godfather abused me. This will always remain a question mark, even as his words attempted to nurture the crop of Catholic faith in the world. In and around my conversation with Sister B, the questions swirled as did forgiveness and the desire to live free. There is a grace spoken throughout these years and continues to speak. God lives. God is. God loves.

The Third Step of AA states: "Made a decision to turn our will and our lives over to the care of God as we understood Him." It is when we try to make our will conform with God's that we begin to use it rightly. To all of us, this was a most wonderful revelation. Our whole trouble had been the misuse of willpower. We had tried to bombard our problems with it instead of attempting to bring it into agreement with God's intention for us. To make this increasingly possible is the purpose of AA's Twelve Steps, and Step Three opens the door. Once we have come into agreement with these ideas, it is really easy to begin the practice of Step Three. In all the times of emotional disturbance or indecision, we can pause, ask for quiet, and in the stillness simply say: "God grant me the serenity to accept the things I cannot change, courage to change the things I can, and wisdom to know the difference. Thy will, not mine, be done."

My pastor was worldly, sensitive, and highly emotional. He had a sharp tongue. He was soft, neither feminine nor athletic. He was confident, brilliant, a Harvard man. He had lost his father when he was just five. He was close to his mother, who lived to see him be ordained a priest. I have no clear idea whether he ever abused other young boys or men. I knew the confusion from my own household of how there can be caring and kindness and in the next instance violence between my parents. It's something many abuse victims are weighted by—someone who seemingly cares for you met with someone who abuses you. It is an anguishing combination. Earlier in this book, I quoted the statistic from a 2003 National Institute of Justice report, that "3 out of 4 adolescents who have been sexually assaulted were victimized by someone they knew well." That is, whether they are family, extended family, neighbors, teachers, or priests. Trusted by churches, education systems, parents. I was too young to realize the magnitude of the toll, the psychological disarray that would continue to stain me.

When, as a grown man in the second half of my life, I moved with fortitude to a willingness to forgive this priest, a peace finally entered my heart. A dissolution of anger. Yet the hurt remains even as I feel freed.

> *So they put a sponge soaked in wine on a sprig of hyssop and put it to his mouth. When Jesus had taken the wine, he said, "It is finished." And bowing his head, he handed over the spirit.*
> —From the Passion of our Lord Jesus Christ according to John (18:1–19:42)

Only our God, Father, Son, and Holy Spirit, knows the reasons why we act the way we do, why we stray, why we wound, why we do not seek to understand, why we take, force, and demand human affection and sexual pleasure even if it may hurt another. And only in this God who loves me and loves those who have hurt me can forgiveness find freedom.

For me, touching the raw wood of the Cross was a heavy price to pay. Even as I write this, I cannot regret this. I had to somehow learn from it to move on to love with hope, one day at a time. This is something I said to Sister B as we shared our stories.

With the teacher, I simply found the strength to end it. The situation. The violence. My youth. I was clear that the taking of me was wrong. It was arranged and expected, often in a car at a beach. In darkness.

With the priest, there was less violence, full body hugging, touching, and masturbating until he ejaculated. The push and pull of wanting to please him, desperately wanting to be accepted and cared for in the great gap of losing my father, I continued to look for him.

A half-century removed from this, I am able to understand consensual adult mutuality in LGBTQ sexual behavior, however people identify their gender. But I knew that both the sexual interchanges back then—in their varying degrees of violence and both their harms—were a complete violation of a young boy made vulnerable by the loss of his father and his home life.

Today, after so much pain around abuse and sexual pain and confusion, I have come into myself, with a sexuality that is healthy and mutual, as a heterosexual man married to a loving wife. Our four decades together were no doubt shaped by early trauma, but I have shared love over these decades with a woman of deep faith and sincere affection.

~

Countless victims around the world have their own stories to tell, their own memories within. Shames they carry. And constant questions. Sometimes, too, the experience of mutual loving relationships in adulthood that are healing. I am not unique.

Though those bearing pain often feel they are alone, unique, with their stories. Until I began to meet other victims, I thought I was alone. Some would come up to me after I spoke at an AA meeting, telling me I had just given words to their own story. *Identify, don't compare.* Soon I learned just how many men and women faced what I faced from abusers, either around a church, synagogue, temple, mosque, locker room, scouting tent, acting audition, sports doctor medical evaluation, or in various other places—especially one's own home. Sexual exploitation, abuse, and violence happen everywhere.

By the time I went off to college, circumstances of life changed. Yes, I was on shaky ground, but removed from my abusers. Though I did remain on talking terms with the priest until the time of his death. And only once did I encounter the teacher after many years.

That occurrence happened when we both attended a Mass in 2008 celebrating the fortieth anniversary of ordination of a mutual priest friend. At the time I was new to sobriety, only four years in. As I was preparing to travel to the event, Charlie, my sponsor, cautioned me, suggesting that if I by chance did run into the teacher, I could simply turn and leave the venue. He called it correctly. When I saw the teacher from a distance on the grounds where the cocktail reception followed the liturgy, I immediately became repulsed and bolted for my car to make the drive back to my home in New Jersey from Port Jefferson, New York.

At that time I was in no shape to comprehend just how much abuse had affected me. Getting into my car and escaping was "doing the next right thing" that recovery teaches the addicted person seeking to hold onto the gift of sobriety. For a long time alcoholism held sway to numb the pain and cushion me from looking under the hood. I still had plenty of work to do. Still very raw, I knew I was on the right road.

5

A Violation Thwarted

~

For the gate is narrow and the way is hard that leads to life, and those who find it are few.

—Matthew 7:14

"What hurts me the most," Pope Francis once said, "are the many occasions when I have not been more understanding and impartial."

> In morning prayers, in supplications, I first ask to be understanding and impartial. I then continue asking for many more things related to my failings as I travel through life. I want to travel with humility, with interpretive goodness. But I must emphasize, I was always loved by God. He lifted me up when I fell along the way. He helped me travel through it all, especially during the toughest periods, and so I learned. At times, when I have to confront a problem, I make the wrong decision, I behave badly, and I have to go back and apologize. All of this does me good, because it helps me to understand the mistakes of others. (*Pope Francis: Conversations with Jorge Bergoglio*, by Francesca Ambrogetti and Sergio Rubin)

It was those words of Pope Francis I recalled during the summer of 2022, when I had a remarkable conversation with Erika, an abuse survivor from Sonora, Mexico, and a divorced mother of three young boys. It is not uncommon in conversations revisiting old wounds for new insights to emerge. As Pope Francis said, "[God] lifted me when I fell along the way." Erika showed utter authenticity as she spoke of how God repeatedly lifted her each time she had fallen hard. Very hard. But she never wavered in her love of God. His comfort brought her profound comfort. As we shared our tough paths toward renewal of faith, the time together surprisingly resurfaced a buried experience of mine related to Mexico and my own history of abuse. I was amazed that my encounter with Erika brought forth this incident I had forgotten.

Erika reminded me of just how vulnerable the abused are, once violated, to further violation. And, how profoundly trauma plays on, harms, the mind. As this woman of faith spoke from her heart about understanding the mistakes of others—something, like Pope Francis, that she sought to do—and as the memory surfaced, our discussion underscored for me why I have had difficulty being impartial and how I resist the humility that helps me travel the road to peace.

When you are a victim of sexual violence, impartiality is understandably elusive. How could it not be? Yet what Erika said, as she shared her own discovery, is that finding interior freedom over time is through the work of intentional impartiality, letting go and trusting the God who always loved her, she said, and who loves *all* both in their light and in their darkness.

As she spoke, my recollections went to Mexico. I had crossed into southern Mexico just before dark. The weekend would go fast, but I was glad to take a break from my studies in Guatemala to spend just a little time in Mexico. Steam covered all the bus windows like waxed paper. It was the rainy season. I was in an unknown environment, and the driver, a slight man with deep-set brown Mayan eyes, wore a smile that exuded assurance and warmth. He drove with confidence, even through tough terrain and heavy downpour. It was August 1979, and at twenty-three, I felt free, like a hiker climbing a new mountain. I was so ready to explore Tuxtla Gutiérrez. My guidebook stressed that visitors must take in the nightlife. So after checking in to the hacienda in the heart of the city that offered guestrooms the size of subway cars—long, narrow, yet inviting—I could not wait to sample what the city had to offer.

The music coming from the club sounded more like rock and roll than mariachi. As I got closer to the entrance, I could make out the familiar tunes of the Rolling Stones. I walked into a dark hallway making my way past couples standing under dim spotlights making out, men kissing women, men kissing men, women kissing women. I reached the bar, which was full of people—a mixture of Mexicans and tourists, I presumed. I snaked through to the bartender, ordered a scotch, and found a stool to lean on. The music was louder now than when I first came into the club; I could not hear anyone talking; I could only see their mouths moving. In this section, the place was as dark as my black alligator shirt—the Izod I loved that fit me like an old shoe, broken in just right.

Next to me, a stocky Mexican guy with long, wavy black hair in a ponytail in his forties appeared out of nowhere. I hadn't noticed him when I had made my way to the bar. He ordered a tequila, winked at me, and moved his head to the left suggesting I follow him. Then, with his left hand, he caressed my right arm, and I heard over the music, "Come with me." I don't know why, but I followed him.

He brought me to a room behind the bar and closed the door. Once inside, he said, "Yo soy Padre Tomas, Father Tom. Amigo. I speak English, so nothing to worry about. I just want to fuck you. You are so good looking, and I need to get my rocks off. Okay? That's all. So relax."

The room had a sofa. He pulled me close to himself and threw us together onto the sofa. He grabbed my crotch and kept saying, "Relax, relax. Won't take long. Enjoy it, enjoy it."

He put his hand down my pants and grabbed me. I pushed him off and jumped up from the sofa. "Father, I have to leave. Let me out of this room."

He said, "Go. Your loss. Go."

I opened the door and ran around the bar and down the hallway past all the people I had seen when I first came in. Once out on the street, I began running as fast as I could toward the place where I was staying.

When I reached my room, I went to my knees and asked God to help me understand what just happened. "Why was this priest who said he was Fr. Tomas there?" "For sex?" "With me?" "With others?" "Was I weak to have gone with him to that back room?" "How did I find the strength to run away?" "God, you were with me, thank you."

Recounting this story with Erika, she identified and repeated a tenet in recovery which binds all seeking sobriety and greater understanding of a Higher Power in one's life: *Identify—Don't Compare.*

Erika told me her own story of being abused from the age of five through seven, by a cousin. Then again, from age nine to fourteen, Erika suffered horrible abuse by a priest associated with the parish she attended and where she was an active choir member. She said:

> I played the guitar, really enjoyed being part of the choir. I don't really remember the first time with the priest; he kept a picture of me in his office; he made me feel so special, but

what he did to me was so disgusting. I told my mother I can recall now when I was twelve years old and she didn't believe me and said he—the priest—loves you very much like a father, that this priest was revered, respected, and favored by the bishop in Monterrey.

I found the strength somehow to visit this bishop before I began my studies to be a nun, around turning age seventeen. The bishop didn't believe me and said to me that I better be careful, implying that I was a bad person. I felt he was blaming me; I felt re-victimized and re-traumatized.

I left confused and saddened but still feeling a pull to study to be a religious sister, I began what I hoped would be a fruitful vocation path toward being a consecrated woman within the Legionaries of Christ, an international order very familiar in Mexico since its roots were embedded in my native country, having been founded by Fr. Marcial Maciel in Mexico City to form Catholic leaders especially in Latin America. It really didn't hit me about Maciel's horrid past abuses and removal from leading Legionaries by the Congregation for the Doctrine in 2006 until I traveled to Rome as part of studies in 2014 and took part in a seminar.

I happened to meet a priest investigating crimes of clerical abuse in the Church who had spoken with another Mexican woman about her past abuse. He offered to meet me in confidence where I could share my story with him. I remember how kind he was and how he listened to me for a few hours. He asked me to follow up with a letter and summarize everything including my meeting with the bishop and how I was not believed and felt threatened.

This whole experience gave me the strength to leave my studies and go into education, becoming a teacher, marry, and have children. I learned that a little after a year I had sat down with the priest in Rome and sent my letter that the priest who had abused me had passed away, but that the bishop was forced by Rome to retire, that he was very angry but complied with the directive.

I am convinced that my continuing to stay in the Church, go to Mass, and participate in the sacramental life of the Church allowed me to never doubt that Christ was by my side, that He was always with me, that through His suffering, I wasn't alone, that He suffered with me by dying on the Cross, that God, father, Christ, son, Spirit, holy, accepted my anger, my wounds and would heal me in His grace, His love for me and for all victims.

Today, I have received an annulment. My wedding in effect was not valid, I was in many ways a victim again during my brief marriage, but my gratitude is rich in the gift of life of my three little boys. God has always been with me and is with me today more than ever. I truly am a survivor.

Reflecting on Erika's faith and journey, I am reminded of the words of Gerard Manley Hopkins, the English Jesuit poet: "The world is charged with the grandeur of God." At no time in her journey did Erika lose hope in just how much God was always present and how God continued to embrace her with indelible love, especially in the depths of her trauma.

To learn from and share with Erika was reassuring as we spoke of our mutual connection to the Bread of Life, how the Eucharist remained in our lives even when we were wounded by priests of the Church and all that had happened to us by being sexually abused. Throughout, the Eucharist remained life-giving and offered us a road toward healing. Beyond the hierarchies of the Church, beyond the human failures. By understanding our suffering in Christ, we came to believe in the mystery of his suffering for us.

From Erika I learned what those words of St. Paul to the people in Corinth truly meant: "So whoever is in Christ is a new creation: the old things have passed away; behold, new things have come" (2 Corinthians 5:17).

6

Thy Will Be Done

A past grace, recalled in memory, still retains something of the original experience, though the effect produced by the remembrance of this communication was received, yet when the communication is recalled, there is a renewal of love and an elevation of the mind to God; this is consequently a great grace, for those on whom God bestows it possess within themselves a mine of blessings.
—St. John of the Cross

The last time I saw my mother was in June 1991 in Port Jefferson, Long Island. I had driven from New Jersey on a Sunday of torrid heat after attending Mass. I made my way over the George Washington Bridge at noon, lucky the traffic was lighter than normal and even luckier that the air-conditioning still worked in my car.

I glanced at my watch. I would arrive in about two hours. The light of day shot through the windows of the car, providing just enough warmth for my body to handle the forced artificial air, but at the same time the sun's beams ensnared me in a lonely muse. My restlessness and wandering mind took some breaks of calm as I listened to a cassette of Mozart's Piano Concerto No.

21, making the drive—this inevitable journey—more bearable.

When I arrived, the hospital room was still, and the mid-afternoon sun filled the chamber through one large window above the courtyard to the west. The walls were painted a lovely soft green—the same shade of fescue weathered by the constant salt mist near the ocean dunes sixty miles east where I was raised. My mother was alone, lying on her back, eyes shut, breathing rhythmically. The sounds reminded me of her graceful freestyle strokes outside the breakers at the beach where I had watched her swim and learned from her to respect the insidious currents beyond the waves. A light, ecru blanket covered her. She had no hair; her weight was ninety-six pounds, and she was, the oncologist had told me, unaware of anyone or anything.

Earlier that summer, I had visited my mother as she was in hospice, where she lay in a hospital bed placed in the living room, with enough space to accommodate hospice furniture and a respirator. I watched as my sister changed her incontinence products near the shelf of adult diapers. I was astonished that she never complained about her befallen duty. And surprised even more by my own patience in the few times I was called on to change the diapers.

In this same room, thirty years prior, I had a front-row seat to another scene playing out when I watched my mother and father kick each other to shreds.

Now, in her swaddling clothes, I was touching her. There was no fight. However strange the current circumstance was, being with her in the moment felt right. Mysteriously, we two were dying together, and the pain was beyond description. I was feeling a profound loss, even as I despised most of what my mother represented. Now the breast cancer had gone to her bones and brain. Her demons vanished.

Now in that hospital room as I stood beside my mother, I reached for her left arm under the blanket. I caressed it softly with my right hand and felt the warmth of her skin. She looked peaceful, and I spoke quietly telling her that I was glad to see her. I don't know if she could feel my touch or if she was able to hear me talking to her.

I then stood in silence for forty more minutes, continuing to stroke her arm and, at times, the top of her head. Her eyes remained closed; not tightly, because when I leaned down, I could see just a little bit of the whites under her lids. She appeared to be meditating.

Suddenly, my mother opened her eyes and looked upward, perhaps unaware of my presence next to her, and began to speak the Lord's Prayer with a piercing clarity. By the time she reached "thy will be done," tears were streaming down my face as I steadied my grip on her arm. When she finished the crescendo, "for thine is the kingdom, the power, and the glory, now and forever. Amen," I fell into her chest sobbing, my tears now uncontrollable. When I looked up, I saw that her eyes were completely closed. And she breathed in the same manner I encountered on first entering the room.

Drained and in awe of what I had just experienced, I left the hospital. My mother never woke again, never spoke again. The following day she died.

7

Descent into Hell

~

Depression is a disorder of mood, so mysteriously painful and elusive in a way it becomes known to the self—to the mediating intellect—as to verge close to being beyond description.

—William Styron

Alcoholism is a family disease. It is often noted in the medical addiction community that one has the "gene," a predisposition to addiction if coming from a family where addiction is rampant. For me, this was certainly true.

After my mother died, I continued to drink daily and heavily for another fifteen years until my second DWI arrest. The daily drinking that followed my being raped as a child continued for thirty-five years until October 6, 2004, the day I stopped cold turkey.

No detox, no rehab, I fell into a deep depression and went into a full-blown withdrawal. The physicality of severe addiction cannot be overstated. When a person uses illicit drugs or alcohol to excess, their body gets used to the fake medicine. To suddenly stop using rather than decreasing amounts and easing the process—especially for someone like me who used alcohol for so many years—exacted a heavy toll.

Much like losing a limb, the human body must adjust; the wound has to heal. You need to figure out how to go on living, how to not take things for granted in the new landscape of your life. Long-term addiction is a stranglehold leaving few options for escape. It is only when you hit bottom that you realize the only way out of the morass is to put down the drink or drug. And then, you need to face the pain that caused you pick up the drink in the first place.

My bottom was hard, harder perhaps than it needed to be because I didn't have the benefit of—nor the inclination for—medical support for detoxification. I toughed it out. I prayed and prayed. I felt God was with me to meet the challenge, after all I lived through and knowing I could have killed myself—or others—getting behind the wheel while drunk.

It was a first step, but as you hear in the rooms of AA, to find humility, you first need to be humiliated.

Was it my pride that made me do this alone? Maybe. But I believed part of my cross required feeling what it was like to remove the substance that numbed me for decades. Here's what the First Step of the 12 and 12 (*Twelve Steps and Twelve Traditions*) says:

> Why all this insistence that every A.A. must hit bottom first? The answer is that few people will sincerely try to practice the A.A. program unless they have hit bottom. For practicing A.A.'s remaining eleven Steps means the adoption of attitudes and actions that almost no alcoholic who is still drinking can dream of taking. Who wishes to be rigorously honest and tolerant? Who wants to confess his faults to another and make restitution for harm done? Who cares anything about a Higher Power, let alone meditation and prayer? Who wants to sacrifice time and energy

in trying to carry A.A.'s message to the next sufferer? No, the average alcoholic, self-centered in the extreme, doesn't care for this prospect—unless he has to do these things in order to stay alive himself. Under the lash of alcoholism, we are driven to A.A., and there we discover the fatal nature of our situation. Then, and only then, do we become as open-minded to conviction and as willing to listen as the dying can be. We stand ready to do anything which will lift the merciless obsession from us.

Two months after my arrest and last drink, shaking uncontrollably from vicious anxiety, not sleeping for weeks, I was alone in our master bedroom. Karen took to sleeping in another bedroom. My constant restlessness kept her awake. She needed her sleep to simply function. It was about 2 a.m. as I recall that particular night. There were no lights on in the room and she'd said goodnight to me around midnight. A full December moon illuminated many things around me, and I could see a few photos of our children on the dresser.

I am not sure there are words that exist to describe what it is like to want to kill yourself. That instant had no tangible explanation, and it was just so contrary to what I knew as a human being about the desire to be alive, however taxing your life might be. But I knew at that moment I experienced an overriding urge to not be alive, to go someplace else, away from this world.

"What I began to discover," as William Styron wrote in *Darkness Visible: A Memoir of Madness*, "is that I was going mad, crushingly mad":

With all this upheaval in the brain tissues, the alternate drenching and deprivation, it is no wonder that the mind begins to feel aggrieved, stricken, and muddied thought processes register the distress of an organ in convulsion.

Sometimes, though not very often, such a disturbed mind will turn to violent thoughts regarding others. But with their minds turned agonizingly inward, people with depression are usually dangerous only to themselves. The madness of depression is, generally speaking, the antithesis of violence. It is a storm indeed, but a storm of murk. Soon evident are the slowed-down responses, near paralysis, psychic energy throttled back close to zero. Ultimately, the body is affected and feels sapped, drained.

Lying in a fetal position in the middle of the bed, I tried unsuccessfully not to shake. In the corner next to the headboard, facing the driveway under the half-opened window, I could see my exercise bike, its yellow frame and shiny silver handlebars. The bike appeared cold, this inanimate friend, the winter air chilling it and the entire room. I thought about closing the window as I rocked back and forth, but I couldn't get up. My legs were tucked against my chest, my hands locked on my elbows, arms embracing my knees. I now moved like a top, limbs ready to explode from my twisting tornado body. I felt tremendous pain up and down my legs—sharp, constant, and biting like barnacles under bare feet.

Nearing sunrise, I broke out of the fetal pose I had held for hours and actually was spiraling now on top of the bed. I jumped up and down, the bed becoming a trampoline for my energy. I felt lost. I hit my head several times on the ceiling above, eventually breaking the box spring below the mattress absorbing my out-of-control wildness. The next hour ended when I rolled off the bed into a ball, exhausted against the exercise bike.

Somehow I managed to get up and opened my closet. Light now filled the room from the early sun. I noticed snow falling gently through the closed window next to me. I took a brown leather belt, thick and strong with a large, square silver buckle, the familiar one I wore with blue jeans, from its hook above the tie rack. In an instant, I wrapped the belt around my neck and step-by-step went through the actions as though readying to hang myself. I played this out a few more times, pulling the belt tighter around my neck through the buckle with my dominant right hand until I could feel the tension from my neck up through my arm to my hand.

Then I walked calmly to the exercise bike and wrapped the end of the belt around the handlebars, keeping the belt as it was around my neck. I attempted to lift myself up, balancing my entire body with my left hand and then dropping myself down so the belt would catch in a way that I would hang in the air. There were only a few feet from the handlebars to the floor to negotiate my suicide. Was I serious about killing myself? Was this really a suicide attempt? Maybe. Maybe raw desperation. But something was going on. I was awake, but it all felt like I was dreaming.

I stopped, went downstairs to the kitchen. Snowflakes falling outside the windows along my path to the drawer next to the stove looked like angels staring at me. Illusions, hallucinations, delusions are all part of a mental breakdown, detoxing, a frenzy that defies reality.

I found the butcher knife resting on the right side of the drawer, alone, its blade faced downward. Grabbing the thick black handle, I pulled it out tightly with my right hand, stood tall, and pretended to thrust it through my chest over and over, at least for three or four minutes. Finishing acting out my attempted suicide, I placed the knife back in the drawer and made my way back upstairs. I climbed onto the bed, reached down to the carpet to my right and pulled the blankets and comforter from the floor, put them over me, and somehow fell asleep for a few hours. Sleep, however short, brought calm.

I went to the 12 noon Mass with a burning desire to go to confession. Something kicked in from the night before. Guilt overwhelmed me. I tried to kill myself or wanted to kill myself. Whatever I went through, I needed to tell someone, hoping to find a priest who would not judge me or tell me I was crazy.

When I recall that afternoon of twenty years ago, I am convinced divine providence works in our lives. I am filled with hope. The kind of hope expressed by my friend and fellow survivor Mike Hoffman, an active, practicing Catholic in the Archdiocese of Chicago. In an email to me about his story of abuse by a serial abuser priest, he wrote about meeting Cardinal Francis George:

> Mark, it was December 2008, I had the opportunity to meet one on one with Cardinal Francis George. It took over a year to meet with the Cardinal because he was battling cancer and in treatment. I understood this certainly given his health. But I cannot begin to tell you how truly pastoral he was, how he apologized to me on behalf of the Archdiocese, really on behalf of the Church.
>
> George had a reputation of being rather conservative but when it came to the sexual abuse issue, I can only say that he got it right, that in that encounter with him, we were two broken men, that it takes dialogue to heal, that his apology was heartfelt, that his hurt was genuine, no question about that, and for the first time in my life, all the years after the abuse, I felt free, a real freedom.
>
> I guess what accompaniment is, what Pope Francis talks about, I went through it with the Cardinal before he passed, and I had a choice as a survivor, and that was to stay active, become more involved in the Church, that is what I wanted and before Cardinal George died he supported and helped finance the Healing Garden we have in Chicago for victims, survivors, for anyone to come and be reminded that *we can heal, that those abused do have a voice* and can be part of the Church, that many yearn like me to stay in

the Church despite having gone through so much pain.

Again, the experience I had was for me an extraordinary pastoral moment, it was feeling Christ alive in me through the love I felt from Cardinal George in that room, across a coffee table, just taking in his apology and realizing I could be free and go on, that my faith would grow in new ways. It was providential. A turning point. I am forever grateful.

That late Sunday afternoon of December 5, 2004, I hoped I would be successful and find a priest to hear my confession. I drove to the Jesuit Loyola Retreat House in Morristown, New Jersey, about ten miles from my home. I still had the driver's license that the court would come for some months later.

When I arrived at the stately mansion, I stood at the front door and pressed button #29. I have no idea why I chose that particular doorbell. I pressed again. Within a few minutes, a deep voice came through the speaker asking, "Can I help you?"

I said, "Yes, are you a priest?"

"Yes, I'm Father Ed Nagle, how can I help you?"

"Father, my name is Mark, can you hear my confession?"

"Yes, Mark, of course, I will buzz you in, come up the stairs and after you enter, I will meet you at the top."

"Okay Father, thank you."

After finding the words to share with Fr. Nagle some of my story, I realized that I was in the company of a man who seemed to understand what I had been through. At one point, he gently interrupted me and said, "Mark, I allow myself one sip of wine a day, when I say or attend Mass—I have been in the AA program for thirty-three years."

I could not believe what I was hearing, and I recall saying, "Father Ed, how did I wind up here right now and find you, discover someone who has lived a sober life so long and a priest at that!"

He simply replied, "The Holy Spirit knows what he is doing, I suppose, let's chalk it up to that."

I detected a quick Irish wit in his warmth and response. And he proved a good listener. Fr. Ed heard my confession and blessed me.

Looking back at that moment of desperation in my life, I understood him to be deeply synodal.

> *To be synodal is to walk together with another person, to listen authentically in order to understand the other with whom you encounter along the human path, both in joy and pain. Fr. Ed modeled the synodal way by his faithful humility as a fellow member of AA—a true disciple of Christ, our shared Higher Power.*

Over time we did our best to keep in touch. And when Ed passed a few years back in Buffalo, New York, where he was serving in a parish, I felt the void. I also felt the gratitude he and I both knew was at the heart of the recovery journey, especially one for us where Jesus Christ continued to be our Higher Power. As one Protestant minister and recovering alcoholic, A. Philip Parham, prayed in his 1987 devotional, *Letting God,* "Lord Christ, help me to be at ease with others and with their ways of recovery. Keep me from my own harsh judgments of others in recovery. Amen."

Just two days after Fr. Ed Nagle heard my confession, desperation struck. The demons took over, and I could not fight them off. I was lost, again on the brink of suicide. Alone in my corner corporate office. The sun had set. Others gone, at home. It is just me.

The digital clock's ruby numbers, bright like a summer sunset, startled me from the fetal position in which I had put myself. I was under the smooth, durable, mahogany desk where on any given corporate day, my size twelve would easily touch the carpet beneath me while I played executive. It was 7:23 p.m. That meant it was 4:23 p.m. in Los Angeles. The voices on the speaker box above me somewhere were faint and distant. I wasn't sure who was on the phone, and I couldn't recall dialing the conference call number to enter the conversation.

When the clock read 7:41, I stared at the numbers, no longer ruby colored, but pink as the vestments worn by priests throughout the world on Gaudete Sunday—the third Sunday of Advent in the liturgical year, marking the coming of Christmas—a time for rejoicing with the Lord's birth drawing near.

I was not rejoicing. The clock turned 7:53. Voices continued to shout from that speaker box on top of the desk. I stretched my right arm out from the twisted cocoon I was in, breaking the shelter I had fashioned for a moment. With my index finger pointing into the pitch-darkness, I managed somehow to push a button that silenced everything. I was going mad. Without question I was in the clutches of full-blown depression, beyond description. Two months to the day since my second DWI arrest and last drop of alcohol after drinking daily for thirty-five years, madness struck.

Still perched under my desk, my hands shuffled back and forth together in unison and rhythmically—a perfect harmony. The bottom of my palms began to bleed from the constant rubbing. Even in the obscure light, I could see the blood on the carpet. My hands stung all over, and my legs were asleep as if they were not a part of me. "Why, why, why," I cackled. "Where am I? Who's there?"

The clock read 8:46. Life returned to my legs, and I rose, standing upright like a Swiss Guard in Vatican City. I marched to each window, all four of them, and lowered the blinds one by one until they were all shut tight. The room was lit slightly only by the EXIT sign with its red neon above the door at the far end of the office, some fifteen feet from where I stood.

As those in the field of psychiatry know, visual hallucinations are a clear sign of one decompensating, having a psychotic break. What I saw was an EXIT sign not simply secured to a wall with its red lettering as I lowered each blind one by one, but rather the word EXIT flashing on and off, swirling over me like mosquitos feasting on sweaty skin.

By 9:10, I was weak-kneed and wobbly. My tornado dance ended when I collapsed to the floor. Dizzy, head fogged, body shaking, I was consumed with fierce anxiety, all of me, as I lay there and cried, resuming my fetal position, kneecaps drawn toward my chest. I looked at the clock: 9:41.

I crawled toward the desk. "No," I whispered to myself. "I don't want to kill myself." Exhausted, tears wetting my face, I took a deep breath, turned on the petite brass desk lamp, and dialed. I knew Dave's number by heart.

My early impression of him was that he was good and kind. I don't know why I chose him to be my sponsor since I first entered the Alcoholics Anonymous program just a few weeks prior.

"Dave, I tried to kill myself."

"Mark, what? When? How?"

"Saturday night, a few nights ago. Hanging, I think. Can't really remember."

"Mark, out of my league. I know alcohol, that's it."

"Dave, will I be okay?"

"Yes. Maybe bad withdrawal, but you must get help! Go to the ER. Call Karen. Get there now!"

"Can you come, Dave?"

"Where are you, Mark?" he said.

"I'm in my office and I'm having suicidal thoughts."

"Mark, I can't help you with that, but I can get you to the ER. Stay there, you're at your office, right?"

"Yes."

"Okay. I'll be right there. I live close by. Just ten minutes, twelve. Stay where you are."

"Okay, I'm staying."

"Hang on, Mark."

"Okay, Dave."

"You sure?"

"Yes."

"I'm leaving now."

8

Locked Ward

The acuity of the heart of God comes with the awareness of the presence of God. Once God takes over the heart, there is no one—no child of God in any tradition any-where—who does not have claim to our heart as well to the heart of God. We become our brother's keeper, our sister's best support. Our own hearts, like God's, begin to beat with a heart for the whole human race.

—Joan Chittister, OSB

Dave had vowed to accompany me until it was certain that I would be taken into the psychiatric inpatient unit. By the time— and with Dave's help—I was admitted to the unit, it was nearing sunrise. My heart was broken. God's heart had touched me. Dave left me, drained, assured. Only a few feet from the place where I would be shuttered, I could make out what appeared to be a brilliance of orange, blue, and red streaming through a port-like window near the entrance of the ward, as an attendant pushed me in a wheelchair missing its leg rests. My feet ached and my knees were in spasms from curling them upward using the last of any remaining strength. The chair kept moving.

Dave left, and I had been in the ER, alone and intentionally isolated in a room, for twenty-two hours. A social worker, at some point, broke the silence in that solitary den, barking that I would just have to be patient and wait, the ward was full. After he said that, he was gone. His use of the word *ward* startled me as though it were a flock of barn swallows swooping down at my head.

The wheelchair driver pressed the oversized blue button next to the double-door. As both doors swung inward, the tile below us, green like seaweed, suddenly rose, twirling like flying saucers around me, circling like buzzards sensing prey. Each moving tile resembled a set of owl-black eyes. I forced myself to blink as the tiles began speaking in a rapid cacophony saying:

"You're crazy."—"What troubles you so much?"—"You tried to kill yourself."—"Why do you not want to live?"—"What is wrong with you?"—"You are mad."—"Don't you believe?"— "What do you want?"—"Who are you?"—"You are mad, mad, mad."

In front of the nurses' station now—I remained seated in the wheelchair, shaken, scared. The psychiatrist who greeted me appeared to be in his late thirties, a decade younger than I with a demeanor colder than a February frozen pond: aloof, bossy, and arrogant. He talked too fast and didn't care if I understood or not.

As he crossed in front of me toward the nurses' station to write a note, no doubt about me and my condition, he yelled to the only nurse present: "Put him on 600 milligrams of Effexor! 500 milligrams of Seroquel! 250 milligrams of Ativan so he'll sleep! He's suicidal! Watch him! I'll be back tomorrow."

While of course alcohol had been part of my life daily for thirty-five years, I had never been on any drug in my life. Only Advil for a bad back. That's it. It was now just about two months to the day that I put down the drink cold turkey after my second DWI arrest and everything went haywire.

I needed to be contained. The madness demanded safety. I drank all those years to numb the pain. Death. Rape. Abuse. All too tough to face. I had no idea that what I was going through was a scourge within the Catholic Church. There were others, victims too many to count.

Now, being in a hospital ward as a very sick patient actually gave me the quiet, the embracing solace I required to look inside, to discern, even to pray, to be in a safe haven, even for a little while.

God knew I needed this time-out, a break from the world where the pace of life never stopped, especially when drinking took center stage. Always.

Here I was in essentially a small dormitory for psychiatrically challenged men and women in the aftermath of suffering nervous breakdowns, suicide attempts, piercing anxiety, torching depression. There was only one phone for all of us. Each night I received a call from a Benedictine monk, Father Germain, whom I had known for the better part of a decade.

Father Germain was an accomplished violinist with a wonderful sense of humor, warmth, and sincerity. Old age and poor health had relegated him most of the time to a wheelchair. All the patients knew, while I was their ward mate that the call coming at the same time each night was for me. In unison they would bark, "It's for you, Williams."

After I managed to meander from my bunk to get to the phone near the front desk, Germain would keep to a short call, simply saying, "Mark, I am praying for you, you will be okay, you are loved, stay strong, good night."

Years later, reflecting on my hospitalization, I remember Germain's goodness and wonder if he had some inclination of what I might have gone through. In fact, after his death only five years after my discharge, the school he taught music at had become embroiled in sexual scandal by some priests accused of abusing a few male students. I will never know how this affected him, maybe hastened his passing. Perhaps his nightly phone calls were a sign from God, using this gentle monk as an instrument of faith for me, an added grace at that profound moment when dying outweighed living for me, a beginning of healing, a response to discover just what my wounds were and what I needed to do.

> People come into our lives at unexpected times, even for a short while. But God knows what he is doing; he is always in charge, and in most people we encounter through his grace, we discover hope.

In his book, *Hurting in the Church: A Way Forward for Wounded Catholics,* Father Thomas Berg wrote about what call, what message, the sexual abuse crisis presents for those who were abused:

The most fundamental and basic call within the crisis is the call to holiness, the invitation to follow Jesus more closely, to discover the paradoxical sweetness and joy of looking into the face of the Redeemer and discovering that he is right there with us in our hurt, that by uniting our suffering to his redemptive suffering, ours can take on unfathomable meaning and incalculable value on a spiritual level which defies human comprehension. The healing we can discover in the wounds of Christ is the healing of the meaning and value of suffering. This is something that he—and he alone—can give to our sufferings, when we surrender them to him.

I stayed in a locked ward in the hospital for eight days. I was given heavy psychotropic medications with some intermittent talk therapy, mostly group therapy. While in the hospital, I had MRI scans of my brain and my back. I'm not sure why.

Getting me on meds and into an outpatient arrangement to receive therapy was the goal. There was no real interest in me as a person, or what really was going on that got me to this point in my life.

I had one visitor, though, that I will never forget. It was my then-pastor Monsignor Kenneth Lasch. For about an hour Ken sat with me on a bench in the middle of that locked ward. He was a leading advocate for those abused in the Church, but at that time twenty years ago I hadn't paid much attention to his pioneering healing work. My own trauma kept me silent.

I now know how he himself suffered emotionally by taking on the hierarchy, brother priests, and others in the Church who covered up the sins of predators. "Mark," I remember Ken saying to me, "this is your Gethsemane."

"I feel the agony, Ken. I need to figure this out. Please pray for understanding."

"It will come, Mark," he said. "I know it will come."

～

Something happened the night before I was to be sent home. Earlier that day my roommate, Larry, who had tried to kill himself by drinking a can of Drano, had been discharged. He left with a life-saving tube the surgeon had put in extending from his neck hitched somehow to one of his lungs. He had told me he wished he had not been saved. I liked him. Like me, he was a crushed soul.

"But you, Mark, you're worth it," Larry had said. "You didn't want to kill yourself. You just toyed with the idea. That you mentioned suicide when you hit the ER got you here for help."

Now in the empty room shuffling past his empty cot toward

the bathroom, I fell to my knees, lassoed to the floor like a horse with no fight. I landed softly. My eyes were blinded by a dazzling light that spoke, "You are alive. You needed this break in your life. You are now prepared to face the past. It is time to surrender. I'm with you."

Beginning that night, I developed a strange and peculiar limp in my right leg. The leg would stiffen like wood, and I moved it by dragging it like I was brushing off some mud from the bottom of my shoe. I must have concealed it somehow because none of the staff who looked after me that last night nor the next half-day before the discharge said anything to me nor offered any question or comment. Yet, I clearly limped, even, at times lunging forward as though in a spasm, as though I were being shoved from behind.

～

Karen, my wife of twenty-three years, came to the hospital to sign the discharge papers. She came into my room and sat next to me on my bed. Her look of kindness pierced me. Taking my hands into hers, she said, "I love you, you are going to be okay, we will get through this together." By the time we left that December day in the late afternoon, I had been hospitalized, locked up in a ward for eight days, on heavy psychotropic medication, and with a pronounced limp. We made our way to the parking garage. It seemed winter arrived since the night I came to the ER. The air was biting. *Does a person feel colder when drugged?* I wondered.

On the way from the hospital toward Morristown, about a ten-mile drive, where we would do a little Christmas shopping and pick up a bite to eat, Karen kept reassuring me: "Mark, you are such a good man, loving husband and father, we are going to get through this, I know you will find health, I know God is with us."

I recall shaking in the car as we parked, experiencing a twitch—my body unable to be still. We started walking near The Green. I dragged my right leg as if it were asleep, and I began to lunge and bang a shoulder into trees, parked cars, garbage cans. I could not control whatever lurched me forward.

When we arrived home in Mendham after our time in Morristown, all I wanted to do was lie in bed, away from all. The depression was as deep as the sea. When I attempted to sleep, I found some peace in my body; the twitching remained but lessened as I lay. Bringing my knees to my chest in a fetal-type position seemed to bring a little calm, but something inside kept fighting to escape my skin. The anxiety felt fast, like a car out of control. The lack of control was fierce and overwhelming.

I was discharged into the real world with an order to see an individual psychiatrist for follow-up medication and a referral to an outpatient clinic for psychotherapy. Neither went well. I did not care for the shrink; he was cold, crude, and uninterested. For the first weeks he kept me on the same meds, then began experimenting with others. During this time, my limp became more pronounced. This psychiatrist noticed it, noting something must be going on neurologically. He ordered another brain scan MRI. This was followed by appointments with a neurologist and a different psychiatrist. Again my medications were changed.

Depression set in deeper, sucking at me like quicksand. I hated facing another day in this state. Everything and everybody didn't matter. I was a shell ready to crack. I needed to find something and someone to help me.

9

Diagnosis

Let us then with confidence draw near to the throne of grace, that we may receive mercy and find grace to help in time of need.

—Hebrews 4:16

It was a glorious October day, the kind with a certain crispness in the air that reddens your face and makes you come alive. Traveling on business, I planned to meet my friend Tom in Phoenix later that day. This would be the first time in my career I was working sober. I got in early enough that there would be plenty of time to have dinner and plan our next day. We worked well together conducting workshops around leadership. It was always fun.

This time was different. I hadn't had a drink, but I wasn't really sober yet. I was what AAers call a dry drunk. It had only been two weeks prior that I'd gotten my second DWI citation, and since that night, an anxiety I had never before experienced and couldn't shake stayed with me. Self-medication with alcohol was no longer an option.

As the plane took off, and as I looked out over the New York City skyline, my thoughts raced with emotion. I began to cry.

I felt something profound but did not know what it was. I did know that I had changed, but I didn't know I was being called to change. The anxiety was fierce; the temptation to ask for a drink overwhelmed me. Previously, I would nestle into that first-class seat and get a drink. Usually I already would have had a couple in the lounge prior to boarding. For a long time I was powerless over alcohol. Now, I had lost my dear friend—booze.

I arrived in Phoenix that afternoon, and then as the day came to a close, the October sunset was magnificent. God's painting of purples and oranges danced over the hills surrounding the city. I felt a kind of pervasive calm. Following dinner with Tom, we mapped out our workshop for the next day, I found a taxi and asked the driver to take me to an address on the outskirts of the city. The taxi dropped me off at a middle school, where an AA meeting was shortly to begin.

The following day, after a lovely southwestern lunch on the terra-cotta patio, Tom and I made our way into the main ballroom for the keynote address. I was looking forward to hearing Ann Richards, the former governor of Texas. She was radiant, funny, and true to form—blunt, calling it as she saw it. What struck me most in her talk—as if God had sent this message to me at this time in my life—was her openness about her own battle with alcohol. She talked about the greatest gift she had: her sobriety. To all of us present she said, "The greatest trait of a leader is to be true to oneself and to be honest with oneself. All else pales, and all else falls into place if you take this road."

After her talk I worked my way through the crowd toward the stage to thank her. She looked straight at me with her morning-sky blue eyes. Right into me. And somehow her expression reached me. I experienced a moment of clarity.

I thanked her and told her that I had just come into the AA program. Without any hesitation, she shot back, "Forget all I said up there and remember this and only this: It is one day at a time." My recovery journey was taking form, and God had sent me a guardian angel, one day, one person, one step at a time.

A few years after I had met her in Phoenix, Ann Richards died. I wept as I read her obituary in the *New York Times*. To me, she was like the poor woman who brought perfumed oils for our Lord, pouring them over his head, presciently understanding the suffering and dying her savior, Jesus Christ, would soon go through.

My recovery journey had just begun. I had no idea what was to come. Being told by Ann to focus on "one day at a time" was prophetic. She also knew I had to die, hit bottom, touch a living death in order to experience the Cross more fully, more completely than ever before. I had work to do if I was to truly embrace what others said in the AA meeting rooms about being joyous and free.

My rock bottom had not yet come. There was a toll to pay, no "easy pass" to the other side. My Gethsemane had come. My Calvary was near. I felt no serenity, but a recognition and a hope as Ann Richards looked through me, poured perfumed oil all over me with her piercing words, "One day at a time."

No matter what I did, I could not shake the anxiety. The limp I developed became even more pronounced, and for some unexplained reason, I would at times lunge, often trying to brace myself on a piece of convenient furniture, so I would not fall. Often, I fell, hitting the ground, my body folding like a marionette waiting to be propped up. Like some persons who spend years in psychiatric residential facilities, walking, shuffling back and forth practically all day around their compound, there was a time I did the same in our home. For six hours straight I walked in a circle until my feet, which seemed as if they were not even attached to my limbs, cried out in pain from blisters as blood seeped through my socks. I collapsed, finally exhausted, on the leather club chair in the den—one of the rooms along my circular route.

Over the next nine months, I saw nearly a dozen doctors, psychiatrists, neurologists, psychologists, and various clinical social workers in day treatment programs. Almost everyone tried or recommended another type of psychotropic medication. Nothing worked. I had MRIs of my brain and my back. I continued to shake, twitch, and lurch. My right leg and even my penis, at times hurt with a sharp pain moving through me like driving rain. No matter what medication I was on, I still couldn't walk properly, my right leg dragging behind me.

The pains would come and go; my skin felt, all over, as though thorn bushes were raked across my body. Only a succession of hot showers would provide some comfort.

Strangely and profoundly, I kept experiencing what the Second Step of AA espouses: "Came to believe that a Power greater than ourselves could restore us to sanity." In and through the falling, the pain, I felt increasingly closer to the Lord. I would pray often, repeating the words of Thomas Merton, words my sister Dawn and I put on our parents' tombstone some years back: "Our world without storms and our lives without agony would give us nothing to grow on. Make us glad for stormy weather."

By mid-summer of 2005, I knew the end was near for my corporate job. I just could not do the work I had in the past. I prioritized my health, and holding on to great medical benefits, even as the doctors and associated professionals I had been seeing had no answers. No one could tell me why I could not walk without a limp, why I shook uncontrollably, why I had these intermittent pains.

Their only remedy was to keep trying ever more, ever different, types of meds. I kept praying to God to give me peace, to help me understand what I was experiencing, to help me be myself again.

Where once it was constant, alcohol was no longer an option. Suddenly the obsession was lifted; it was gone. I realized I did not desire to take a drink like I had daily for thirty-five years. I had no explanation for it, but I felt grateful. Even so, I remained depressed, with thoughts of suicide similar to those I had before I went to the ER at the end of 2004. I continued to seek answers.

Having attended Columbia University for graduate school, I was aware of the reputation of the Columbia University Medical Center and its Neurological Institute. I called for an appointment, explaining to the intake person, the best I could, what I had been going through, asking for their help in finding an expert to help put it all together. That's how I was given an appointment to meet with Dr. Paul Greene, a neurologist, in six weeks' time. Getting an appointment was not easy, but I took it and said thank you.

When the time came, I took the subway uptown and found the Neurological Institute near 168th Street and Broadway. I could walk quickly, if I dragged my right leg faster and faster. My leg would follow if I willed it to. Karen had a meeting and planned to drive to the city to join me later.

There were patients lining the corridor and several in adjoining rooms, all seemingly moving and shaking. I felt welcomed. There were others who struggled as I did. I also felt disturbed. Was this the last straw? Would I find out what my condition was? Would it be permanent? Was there hope? Was it brought on by my quitting alcohol? Was it brought on by my not working out? I always had been an athlete, but this past year the pain drove that to a halt. As I waited there with others who couldn't stop shaking, I thought that my limp, simply, had become part of me. It was how I walked.

Dr. Paul Greene was kind, warm, professional, and focused. He met me in his office, along with a colleague—a woman who was a neuropsychologist. As with my two DWIs, there was always another person who served as a witness in the examining room. But I remained focused on what Dr. Greene had to say. Before my appointment, I had sent Dr. Greene a series of MRI images taken in the previous year. He asked me to come out to the hallway and walk down the corridor about thirty feet and then back to him. My right leg dragged along the linoleum. I turned around like a ship pulling into a tight slip ready to anchor and hustled back to him, dragging my leg faster to show him how pronounced this limp of mine was.

We returned to his office after my dance. And he looked at me with a clarity I had not experienced since Ann Richards told me in Phoenix to forget all she had said and to only say to myself, "One day at a time."

"Mark, there is nothing physically wrong with you," he said. "There is something psychologically going on, perhaps something you've never dealt with, never talked about; some trauma, which is manifesting itself in the physical symptoms you are experiencing. Mark, it is real; I know you are not making this up. I understand, and I am going to make a referral right now to my colleague, Dr. Dan Williams, one of the leading experts in the world on 'conversion disorder,' which I believe there is no question you have, and I want you to see him in the next forty-eight hours, the sooner the better."

After almost a year, I was finally diagnosed: A conversion disorder—a deep psychological condition that manifests itself with very demonstrative, often bizarre, strange, and peculiar physical symptoms.

At times over the years, I would recall the abuse. For some reason, I never named it as such. I didn't give it the clarity of diagnosis. I didn't look at it with a direct gaze, the way Ann Richards, the way Dr. Greene had, and attributed what I went through as *abuse*.

Perhaps the combination of the power of the mind to deny with the excessive use of alcohol served to protect me from the shame and the deep wounds of the abuse. But did I forget? Why did I not admit the pain and the trauma of the past sooner? I don't know the answers.

Richard Rohr has often quipped that more spirituality happens in church basements during an AA meeting than upstairs in the main church during a liturgical service! In *Breathing under Water: Spirituality and the Twelve Steps*, he writes:

> The foundational ways that I believe Jesus and The Twelve Steps of AA are saying the same thing but with different vocabulary:
> We suffer to get well.
> We surrender to win.
> We die to live.
> We give it away to keep it.

Of course, the journey really never ends. And my journey is just beginning. To me, the way of the cross continues to be the life, the soul, and the love of becoming whole. The maturity and wisdom that come with time are the reason these words of the truth of my life come easier now.

To face that darkness, I needed years of sobriety, reflection, and a deepening faith. And while others, out of their deepest pain, justifiably couldn't look to the Church—where their abuse came from, and where support for survivors has been denied, ignored, or been so devastatingly long in coming—I knew I somehow needed to participate in praying, and supporting Pope Francis whose heart appeared to be broken, for victims across the world hurt and abused in the Church. Where previous popes remained silent, he listened, he spoke, and he began to crack the doors of religious power open—for change.

Pope Francis's modeling the Good Samaritan helps me to not stay trapped as *victim*, but to seek to live as a *survivor*. A deacon friend of mine, an ordained African American Catholic, whose journey was from the Jim Crow South to a northeastern pulpit, has an understanding of injustice and deep violation of the human heart. He once expressed to me, "You are an instrument, and God wants you to be one for himself as he works in you to help others."

While I've been humiliated, I'm not sure I'm yet humble enough to be this instrument, but in a continuance of grace and freedom, I received my friend's words as a call to increase my faith for this work done only by grace.

As Ann Richards and the AA community would say, just one day at a time. That is all, to live the Good News one day at a time. The Gospel story of suffering, dying, and rising again acknowledges that when we fall, we must be open to heal, to face the truth of our brokenness.

For our brothers and sisters, especially those whose spirits have been isolated and crushed through abuse, I seek to make things right, to console, and to love, and the Church needs to address these too. It is a call in me that is ever growing. Pope Francis urges us to *go out to the field hospital and help the wounded.* The joy of love, the service of love, is an invitation for us all, especially the abused within the human family. Jesus knew loss and pain. At his friend Lazarus's tomb, he wept. And facing his cross and knowing what was to come, he wept great drops of anguish, tears, and blood in that Garden of Gethsemane. We who have experienced the garden of tears have been invited to face our darkest truths and biggest hopes, invited now to rise from the weeping and see the freedom set before us.

10

Gentle Expert

I am the true vine, and my Father is the vine grower. He takes away every branch in me that does not bear fruit, and every one that does he prunes so that it bears more fruit. You are already pruned because of the word that I spoke to you. Remain in me, as I remain in you. Just as a branch cannot bear fruit on its own unless it remains on the vine, so neither can you unless you remain in me.
—John 15:1–4

Dr. Williams was—as Dr. Greene had informed me earlier—one of the world's leading experts on conversion disorder. A psychiatrist, he taught on the subject, as well as wrote and lectured on the condition. Arguably, the disorder, which I was to find out, is the most severe form of what are called *somatoform disorders*. In the eleventh edition of *Merritt's Neurology,* edited by Lewis P. Rowland, Williams contributed the following:

> Somatoform disorders are frequent challenges to neurologists, psychiatrists, and other physicians for differential diagnosis and treatment. The essential features of somato-

form disorder are physical symptoms that suggest a general medical condition, but are not adequately explained
by any general medical disorder, by the direct effects of
a substance or by some other psychiatric disorder. The
symptoms must cause clinically meaningful distress or
functional impairment.

By definition, the symptoms are not intentionally produced, so distinguishing them from factitious disorders
and malingering. Furthermore, somatoform disorders differ
from "psychological factors affecting a medical condition,"
for example, stress-induced hypertension, insofar as there is
no diagnosable general medical condition that adequately
accounts for the physical symptoms.

My wife and I crossed the George Washington Bridge on our
way to the appointment; it was a warm and muggy August morning. The heat was calming. My body, as if in a sauna, enjoyed the
penetrating hot air. I saw the Manhattan skyline as the Empire
State Building rose to the sky, covered by soft clouds floating in
the summer heat.

Had I lost the life I had known? What was next? Will I ever
walk again normally? These were questions I shared with Karen
as we drove. As we arrived and then waited for Dr. Williams, she
gave me a calm, we'll-figure-it-out look. Karen's sincerity always
brought me comfort, no more so than at this moment when I
felt so lost. A woman of extraordinary depth and abundant faith,
she is someone who went through her own dark valley when she
was a young adult. To me, she's always had a presence, like Mary
of Magdala, the first evangelist to the disciples, telling them the
mystery of the resurrection before they themselves realized it.
And in that spirit of change, resurrection, mystery, and hope,
Karen told me that God was with me, that peace would come,

that I would get well, that our love was what mattered. In all our years together, her words always hit the mark, brought assurance, hope.

As we continued waiting, I closed my eyes for short time. And now other words came to me, words of a childhood Gaelic song originating from the words of St. Patrick's Breastplate written in the eleventh century. The words continued to repeat within me, and the tune I later learned was called "Morning Has Broken," the words of the third verse coming into me so profoundly:

> Mine is the sunlight, mine is the morning,
> born of the one light Eden saw play,
> praise with elation, praise every morning,
> God's re-creation of a new day.

Williams, a slight, small man, walked toward us with a bounce of confidence. The African American guard nearby smiled; young residents, mostly Asian in their starched white lab coats, ran to catch the next elevator. I immediately felt this doctor's warmth and concern, his genuineness, his purposefulness in helping and consoling.

He understood the pain I was in; the first handshake convinced me of that. Already he was different from all the other medical people I'd consulted with before I met Dr. Greene. I was in the company not only of a talented physician, but I perceived him to be another angel sent from God, a man of unquestioned goodness. I looked at Karen, who shared in a glance her sense of him too. A first impression that lasted. Even my shaking body paused during this introductory encounter.

In Step Three of AA, we make a decision to turn our will and our lives over to the care of God. We must take action and let go of the self-will and allow others to help, including those who come into our lives sent by God and who personify God through the goodness of their actions.

In turning my life over to God, I opened myself to Dr. Williams's help. As he reached my interior darkness, he saw my desire to stay in control. He saw my limp and how my body shook uncontrollably. Yet, instead of judgment, he offered kindness, confirming what his colleague, Dr. Greene, had expressed, that "What I was feeling was real, very real."

AA Step Three tells us:

> We'll listen politely to those who would advise us, but all the decisions are to be ours alone. Nobody is going to meddle in our personal independence in such matters. Besides, we think, there is no one we can surely trust. We are certain that our intelligence, backed by our will power, can rightly control our inner lives and guarantee us success in the world in which we live. This brave philosophy, wherein each [person] plays God, sounds good in the speaking, but it still has to meet the acid test; how well does it actually work? One good look in the mirror ought to be answer enough for any alcoholic.

I trusted Dan Williams. Without the time to build a relationship, I knew he was my last hope. In his office, together we peeled the onion. When I told him I had been on eleven different psychotropic medications within the past year, he just shook his head in disbelief. Alongside my immediate trust in this doctor came an immediate recognition I needed to forgive myself, and others perhaps. A calm enveloped me, even as memories rose and were examined together. My buried pain began to find words.

> Forgiving does not mean forgetting. Or better, in the face of a reality that can in no way be denied, relativized, or concealed, forgiveness is still possible. In the face of an action that can never be tolerated, justified, or excused, we can still forgive. In the face of something that cannot be forgotten for any reason, we can still forgive. Free and heartfelt forgiveness is something noble, a reflection of God's own infinite ability to forgive. If forgiveness is gratuitous, then it can be shown even to someone who resists repentance and is unable to beg pardon. Those who truly forgive do not forget. Instead, they choose not to yield to the same destructive force that causes them so much suffering.
> —Pope Francis, *Fratelli Tutti, On Social Fraternity and Social Friendship*

As I was leaving the doctor's office, I thought of an event that happened three decades prior that was in the news and Catholic media. Jean Donovan, a Maryknoll-trained lay missionary, was brutally raped and murdered in El Salvador along with her three fellow church women, just a few months after Archbishop Oscar Romero was gunned down while celebrating Mass in San Salvador. She had been a dear friend studying with me in Huehuetenango, Guatemala, before she left for El Salvador. Together with other students we attended Mass in the quaint church, typically filled with ornate wood carvings magnificently painted with pastel colors. The church was always packed with the wonderful, faithful Indigenous people of this resplendent place nestled in the northern mountains of Guatemala, living within unjust economic and political systems in a country of diverse people, where over twenty languages were spoken.

I understood them to be as the people of the Beatitudes that Jesus's Sermon on the Mount reached: "Blessed are the meek, for they shall inherit the earth." These people *were* the living Beatitudes.

As Karen and I walked out of the medical building, I recalled this one liturgy, in particular, where a young priest whose name I don't recall—tall and towering over all the congregation like a statue coming alive—preached so robustly and strong, almost shouting to the people, as many newborns around Jean and me wailed, "Nosotros estamos viviendo en Jesucristo!" *We are living in Jesus Christ!*

Leaving Dr. Williams's office I felt, and feel it deeply even now, how prophetic his words and presence were.

Never did I feel that more—that we live in Christ, we live, crucified and resurrected in Christ, and that indeed now, we *are living* in Christ—than when Karen and I drove back over the George Washington Bridge. Heading west, the August morning greeted us with more heat, no longer stifling but welcome, renewing.

11

The Cross and the Prayer

~

Then they came to a place named Gethsemane, and [Jesus] said to his disciples, "Sit here while I pray." He took with him Peter, James, and John, and began to be troubled and distressed. Then he said to them, "My soul is sorrowful even to death. Remain here and keep watch." He advanced a little and fell to the ground and prayed that if it were possible the hour might pass by him.
—Mark 14:32–36

After the appointment, as we headed to our car, I noticed Karen parked close to Union Theological Seminary, where one of my favorite spiritual writers, the renowned Jewish theologian Rabbi Abraham Joshua Heschel, taught for many years. So, arriving home, I looked for Heschel's *Quest for God* on the bookshelf in our living room. I opened it to a page I'd highlighted years earlier, where a postcard served as bookmark marking the page. The highlighted passage was one on prayer, undoubtedly meant for this future time, as I read it again now. Heschel penned:

Prayer takes the mind out of the narrowness of self-interest and enables us to see the world in the mirror of the holy.

For when we betake ourselves to the extreme opposite of ego, we can behold a situation from the aspect of God. Prayer is the way to master what is inferior in us, to discern between the signal and the trivial, between the vital and the futile, by taking counsel with what we know about the will of God, by seeing our fate in proportion to God. Prayer clarifies our hope and intentions. It helps us discover our true aspirations, the pangs we ignore, the longings we forget. It is an act of self-purification, a quarantine for the soul. It gives us the opportunity to be honest, to say what we believe, and to stand for what we say. For the accord of assertion and conviction, of thought and conscience, is the basis of all prayer.

The greatest gift for anyone embracing a Christian journey of faith is that unselfishness that Heschel speaks of in prayer. As a Christian, I found this in the utterly unselfish gift of Christ dying as a human being for the sake of others, embracing the cross. I can't quite say how I understood the rabbi's words on prayer echoed the humility of Jesus given for the world, but the mystery of the cross has been life-giving for me. For me and I expect for many others who have chosen a road less traveled, the cross is both symbol and path, paved with stones of forgiveness. All I couldn't hold, forgiven. All the anger I did hold, forgiven.

And I understood the cross also extended beyond my need of forgiveness to what forgiveness shared meant in the words of Jesus, to "forgive those who trespass against us." In the cross, I've been able to not only set myself free, but found a way to set the predator free as well. The cross and all its mysterious forms, its bareness, its beauty, its mystical significance, extended something that in meeting Dr. Williams, in peeling the onion, in being given the words of Abraham Heschel, somehow changed me.

The intersection of a psychiatrist's assurance with a rabbi-scholar's depth in words brought me closer to humility and the ultimate humble act of Jesus dying on a cross for all humanity. In AA's Seventh Step, humility is described as a healer of pain. I couldn't get well myself. I had to humble myself and accept the help of others—especially the help of the one who was nailed to a cross. In doing so, I was on a path to heal.

Henri J. M. Nouwen writes in *With Open Hands*:

Perhaps the challenge of the gospel lies precisely in the invitation to accept a gift for which we can give nothing in return. For the gift is the life breath of God himself, the Spirit who is poured out on us through Jesus Christ. This life breath frees us from fear and gives us new room to live. A man who prayerfully goes about his life is constantly ready to receive the breath of God, and to let his life be renewed and expanded. The man who never prays, on the contrary, is like the child with asthma; because he is short of breath, the whole world shrivels up before him. He creeps in a corner gasping for air and is virtually in agony. But the man who prays opens himself to God and can freely breathe again. He stands upright, stretches out his hands and comes out of his corner, free to boldly stride through the world because he can move about without fear. A man who prays is one who can once more breathe freely, who has the freedom to move where he wishes with no fears to haunt him.

I began to pray into that freedom, prayer after prayer and one in particular that I wrote, "The Ventriloquist," was a beginning to prayer, allowing me to begin releasing my deep-seated burden of fear. I wrote this prayer during my hospitalization, following my nervous breakdown in December 2004, inspired by my daughter Meryl, with whom I began to open up, sharing with her the pain-filled story of those who harmed me and the pain I then lived with.

The Ventriloquist

*Lord, hear my prayer of fear, my wandering, how I've
   hurt my family.*

*Forgive me, dear Brother Christ, for I am lonely and
   afraid and seek you now. And always.*

*I imagine speaking your words—like a ventriloquist—
   with my voice, out loud for all to hear.*

*"No longer do I call you servants, for a servant does not
   know what his master is doing; but I have called you
   friends."*

*Dear Christ, my mother was a drunk; she was beautiful.
She could smoke a cigarette and cook ham at the same
   time.
She was insane, I mean really nuts.
Elegant, tough to the brim.*

*She's in me, I'm in her.
I see it, can even mouth it—like a ventriloquist.*

*Twelve years old, I took the car out for a joy ride.
The officer brought me home, back to Mom.
Pulled over for the first time, long ago.
What has changed? Anything? Nothing really.*

*And then pulled over for the last time. Another DWI,
Lord, why? Can you help me understand?*

My daughter pours the rum to the tip of the shot glass.
She downs it, a true party girl.

Fishnet stockings, eyes caked heavy; ready to go.
Was she heading to where I was, where my mother had
*   been? A drunk?*

Thank God, no.

But my mother haunted her.
Since she was eight years old, she felt that rasping pres-
*   ence.*
Sometimes she panics, I fear that my mother'll rip into
*   her.*
Her hair thick, coarse like my mother's, she does lash out.
She can't help it. I would lash out too. At eight. I did.

Now I am twenty-three years married.
I met my daughter at the parking lot; had lost my wallet.
Later finding it, under the car seat. Stressed out.
Can't remember how old she was. Young.
We walked side by side, and then I told her, "I have a
*   problem."*
And the truth I told hit her hard.

I want to be a good father. She told me that I always
*   was.*
We hugged and cried. Me, who cares for her.
My daughter, who cares about me.
Everything is getting a little clearer now.

Can we, can I, be sober in God's love, not drunk any-
*   more.*

Can his voice become our voice? The true Ventriloquist is
*   God.*

Lord, hear my prayer of fear, my wandering, how I've
*   hurt my family—*
forgive me, dear Brother Christ, for I am lonely and
*   afraid—*
and still I seek you now. And always.

Amen.

12

The Truth Will Out

Jesus went around to all the towns and villages, teaching in their synagogues, proclaiming the gospel of the kingdom, and curing every disease and illness. At the sight of the crowds, his heart was moved with pity for them because they were troubled and abandoned, like sheep without a shepherd. Then he said to his disciples. "The harvest is abundant, but the laborers are few; so ask the master of the harvest to send out laborers for his harvest."
—Matthew 9:35–38

It was Christmas morning, a year since I had been hospitalized. A few hours earlier I'd come from Midnight Mass, tangible, resplendent. As the new day broke, I felt the presence of the Christ child profoundly. That sacred space filled me with a joy I had not felt for what seemed a lifetime. Because of grace, I was present again, alive again, for my family, for me.

A month prior, my second sponsor in AA, Charlie, had asked me: "When was your first drink?" My therapy with Dr. Williams prepared me for questions to come roiling up. For a few moments I couldn't speak. I began to weep. No one had ever asked me that question.

Then he asked me what I was responding to, what was caus-
ing me to cry?

"Charlie," I said. "It's all coming back to me."

"What's coming back?"

"The night of my first drink—when I was raped."

The moment I spoke those words, I felt an uncanny freedom,
a lightness. The sharp pain I had experienced in my leg since
my hospitalization a year previously was gone. In this instance
Freud was right: "Unexpressed emotions will never die. They are
buried alive and will come forth later in uglier ways."

Feeling the lifting of my pain, I looked at my leg, testing it.
No trace of a limp, no dragging my leg like a shackled prisoner.
Telling Charlie the secret I carried loosed the secret that was killing me, that I had been drinking down, a secret my body—my
leg—literally was dragging. Now, clean and sober, I no longer
had to bury the ugly.

One day I shuffled, like a homeless wanderer in my own
home, dragging a leg, the right one, circling the downstairs
for six hours before collapsing on the sofa in the living room,
on my route, from sheer exhaustion. And on this day, speaking with Charlie, I felt a change so immediate that it felt like
freedom in my body. Step Five of the AA program is the pivotal
step where the addicted person has the chance—if he or she is
truly willing—to shed the dark secrets within: We "*admitted to
God, to ourselves, and to another human being the exact nature
of our wrongs.*"

Nearly a year since I had been hospitalized psychiatrically,
resigned from my corporate position, begun to attend AA meetings consistently, found a new sponsor in Charlie, sat back in
the pews, expanded my prayer life, and was seeing Dr. Williams
weekly for psychotherapy and the weaning off unnecessary
psychotropic medication, I was ready to let go of my secret,

the abuse I had experienced by the teacher and priest. A year of emotional and physical cleansing without alcohol in my system was necessary, essential, to finally releasing the ugly that even prevented me from being able to walk as I always had.

> I believe God sends us messengers at the right hour to assist in our healing journey—including mental health professionals and sponsors in recovery.

My body moved into the Fifth Step. Charlie heard it. He saw it. I said it. My loosed leg confirmed it. I admitted to God and to him what had happened to me, the wrong of it, as well as the nature of my wrongs, where I had failed and sought to do better one day at a time. Everything *does* belong, as Richard Rohr wrote.

In the months that followed I began to understand it was up to me with the help of the fellowship in the rooms of AA, with my Higher Power, Jesus Christ, to carry the message and help another suffering alcoholic—and in time, maybe even carry the message to other sexual abuse victims as well.

The Sunday after I found the courage to tell Charlie when and why I had taken my first drink, I attended the 7 a.m. Men's Step AA meeting I had been going to. I mainly listened to learn. Occasionally I would share out loud on a given step.

It was no coincidence, I just knew, and no doubt grace, that this particular meeting happened to be on the Fifth Step. There were some twenty men in this church hall seated in a circle. Each man took a turn and read a paragraph before the entire content of the step was covered. And then the leader opened the time to an open sharing. I recall my share and feeling so free to tell these fellows what happened with Charlie. Most of the men had witnessed the way I walked into this meeting the past several months, and some commented on how today I walked in . . . differently. The truth *does* set you free.

In AA it is said that more will be revealed.

There was man in that group two decades ago, Mark K., a few years older than I, who always shared with a depth that filled me with greater understanding about the plight of those battling addiction doing whatever it takes to stay clean and sober. I hadn't seen Mark K. since that meeting in 2004. I had moved out of this town, found other meetings to attend.

Then, in the latter months of 2023, I happened to run into Mark K. at a meeting in a neighboring village to my new address. We recognized each other right away. We got caught up a bit, and I asked him if he remembered what I had gone through and shared nearly twenty years ago in the meeting.

He immediately said, "Yes, of course, you helped to change my life."

"What do you mean?" I asked.

He took me by my arms and looked directly into my eyes saying: "Look at you, how you walk now, I *do* remember!"

I told him I was writing about my experiences and asked him if he would consider sending me an email about that time, what he had witnessed, what he meant about changing his life. He agreed to share his experience with me, and for others to read. And in an October 12, 2023, email, he wrote:

I had been clean and sober for 22 years, but I certainly wasn't sober. So I returned to AA. It's a program of rigorous honesty and that scared me to death. For 22 years I had lied to myself. Now I had to admit that I was an alcoholic and bare the secrets of my soul. Doing a fourth step by taking a searching and fearless moral inventory and a fifth step, admitting to the exact nature of my wrongs—were tasks that I did not want to undertake but knew that I had to if I were to save myself and my relationship with my wife and daughters. I had the willingness but lacked the courage.

At the time I was attending a Sunday morning men's step meeting and on this particular day the topic was the fifth step. While many people shared, no one made more of an impression than Mark W., who had buried his trauma so deeply along with his shame and guilt that it had not only led him to the depths of alcoholism but manifested itself physically, so painfully that he had lost the ability to walk. In the meeting he recounted his fifth step conversation with his sponsor revealing the nature of the trauma he suffered and the secret he had kept for so long.

I listened, spellbound, as he told us how he broke down sobbing as he let years of guilt and shame pass between himself and his sponsor. He concluded his story with what appeared to me as a miracle. His sponsor, who was there, encouraged him to stand and walk upright, which he did, this time unaided by crutches or cane.

It was not merely the relief of sharing his secret but, more importantly, the forgiveness he obtained for himself and that he was able to extend to his tormentors that enabled him to put down his awful burden and move on to a fulfilling life of sobriety.

Any lingering doubts and fears I had about my own moving forward with my fourth and fifth step work evaporated. No psychiatrist, clergy, doctor or friend had been able to relieve Mark W. of the weight he had carried for years. It was just one alcoholic talking to another about their shared experience that enabled him to forgive himself and those who had harmed him. Now that the wreckage of the past had been put behind him, he was able to experience a spiritual awakening that transformed despair into hope and fear into faith.

I found the courage to change that day and it has transformed my life as well.

I recalled all this that anniversary of Christ's birth that Midnight Mass and the following morning as the fresh smell of breakfast brought us all downstairs. More family would come later to celebrate this anniversary of Christ's birth, but this was the time people shouted, "Wonderful Counselor, Prince of Peace, be with us."

When we left after breakfast, the snow outside was fitting and calming. Now was just our time, the six of us—Karen, the one who stayed near when everyone else left, when I was at my lowest, the one who held my hand, and our four children, true gifts from God: Emily, Meryl, George, and Rebecca. We always had fun opening stocking gifts—small, personal, intimate trinkets. Big presents were not us. So many had far less than we. This was our time for acknowledging we were blessed, fortunate. Looking at them, once we all gathered in our home, I took in the moment fully, as I had never done in the past. And saw them. And they saw me.

Within me was the inner peace of a healing soul. I was surrounded by those who loved me. This was all that mattered. I was sober. I felt free.

I opened a gift from my youngest daughter, Rebecca. She was thirteen then, and for an instant, I recalled being thirteen more than half a life ago. I could not remember that Christmas of my youth, the one just days after my rape. And other holidays that followed blended together during the time of the clerical abuse.

I continued to unwrap her gift, a photo album. I looked up at her and then paged through the many pictures of me happy, as well as many of me drunk. I could tell the difference. The blue in my eyes spoke and did not lie in each photo. Sober, I looked at my eyes across various photos and occasions in the collage of photos put together by Rebecca of our relationship, father and daughter.

I turned back to the front of the book and impeccably glued into place was a letter from her:

Dad,

I don't know if you recall a family therapy session a few months ago in which I clearly told you I had no hope for your condition and state of being. I told you that with courage, for it wasn't easy for me to tell you because at that time that was the bitter truth.

However, over the last few months, you have become someone I knew a long time ago and also like someone I've just met. This person you have become is someone I have hoped for; it's someone who convinces me to simply hope. As a crane is a symbol of hope, I want you to know that you are a symbol to me, and I want to show you that I have also grown as you have as a friend, father and husband. Not only have you been able to make me smile again, but also you have made yourself smile.

Thank you for fighting and clearing the blurred image of hope for my eyes. I love you forever and always.

Merry Christmas, Rebecca Gwen.

Reading the letter, I wept. And wept.
My tears flowed like a river at springtime's thaw.

13

From Victim to Survivor

"My grace is sufficient for you, for power is made perfect in weakness." I will rather boast most gladly of my weaknesses, in order that the power of Christ may dwell with me. Therefore, I am content with weaknesses, insults, hardships, persecutions, and constraints, for the sake of Christ; for when I am weak, then I am strong.
—2 Corinthians 12:9

At times over the months and years that followed, I would think about the abuse and how I lived in denial—never acknowledging, never connecting the abuse to the years of drinking, hiding, shame. Perhaps the power of the mind to deny combined with the excessive use of alcohol served to protect me in a way—or I used it to protect me—from the shame and the deep wounds of the abuse.

Had I been kidding myself? Did I actually forget? Why was it I did not speak the words of my situation sooner?

I don't have the answers. But I do know—or at least have come to understand—that when we feel the most weak and lost, there we might find God, the God who emptied himself into humanity, into suffering, into unjustly being crucified. As I saw it, he was the ultimate victim. Risen, he was the ultimate survivor.

A half century removed from those sexual violations against me, my heart, soul, mind have been released like an eagle, soaring upward from the truth of my situation to the truth *told*, admitting I was abused as a child and minor.

> Sexual violation of a person, male or female, especially a child who is developing emotionally, physically, and sexually, naturally impairs their normal growth. The manipulation, fueled by the abuser's own sexual immaturity, is extremely troubling and wrong. The value of a therapeutic experience in adulthood is invaluable to reach the deep feelings of shame, to heal the trauma that occurred earlier in life. There are countless victims in and out of the Church. Getting help is not just okay. It is so, so right.

But to face this truth, to speak the darkness, I needed to hit rock bottom, something I couldn't do until I was ready, until I was an adult (reasonably) capable of dealing with the pain and the memories. And then, it was only by the grace of God holding me through the pain. A sober person raw and naked to the truth—this was the only path to an authentic life.

In the well-known words of Abraham Lincoln's 1860 speech, "I have been driven many times to my knees by the overwhelming conviction that I had nowhere else to go."

Forced to my knees, I indeed found nowhere else to go. I found humility only by being humiliated. And freedom only by humility. "Whoever exalts himself will be humbled," Jesus said in Matthew's Gospel, and "whoever humbles himself will be exalted" (23:12).

Deborah, my Canadian friend, also an abuse survivor, having gone through horrific sexual abuse by clergy, has been an ongoing example of that humble road, of the work required of journeying from victim to survivor. Once in an email she wrote about that journey, putting it to me this way:

I believe that for healing to occur for the abuse survivors within the Catholic Church, the Church must come clean and be repentant by always remembering abuse survivors in the Prayers of the Faithful at every liturgy and that the Church should have a Mass yearly all around the world for those wounded under the roof of the Church by spiritual leaders.

I really have been struggling with my faith and trust in the Catholic Church, especially now with what is coming out regarding the Indigenous people here in Canada. This has triggered my trauma and lowered again my trust and faith in the Church.

I still faithfully pray and believe in God, but I feel disconnected from the Church, because of this continual breach of trust. But I will make a genuine attempt to attend Mass for the first time in almost four years. I miss the Eucharist. I want the Church to pray for the wounded, show that they care for me. I forgive, but the Church must do more and should do it from their hearts because it is the right thing to do.

In his book *Touch the Wounds: On Suffering, Trust & Transformation*, Tomáš Halík, Czech philosopher, theologian, and priest, captures Deborah's sentiments, her aching, searching heart:

To touch Christ's wounds, not only those in his hands and feet, which tell of his physical suffering, but also "the wound in his side" that struck the heart, is to touch the darkness contained in the cry of one totally abandoned by God.

That wound in the heart is what is testified to by Jesus's words on the Cross that only one of the evangelists had the courage to preserve: "My God, why have you forsaken me?"

My transition *from victim to survivor* has taken time. Over half my lifetime. I have had the good fortune and sustaining peace of mind that come only by holding onto the gift of grace and the gift of sobriety for nearly two decades, gifts both rooted in being loved by Jesus Christ.

As I've said, trauma is the devil. And victimhood is the devil's vice grip. For the still countless victims of abuse, as well as their families, friends, and respective faith communities who continue to suffer, I pray daily.

And among the prayers I offer is this from Scottish theologian John Baillie's *A Diary of Private Prayer*:

Be with me in my silence and in my speech, in my haste and in my leisure, in company and in solitude, in the freshness of the morning and in the weariness of the evening; and give me grace at all times humbly to rejoice in Thy mysterious companionship. Amen.

14

A Friendship Is Born

～

There is no passion to be found playing small—in settling for a life that is less than the one you are capable of living.
—Nelson Mandela

In early September 2018, I attended a talk at Fordham University's Lincoln Center campus in New York City. Cardinal Joseph Tobin, archbishop of Newark, New Jersey, was listed as the speaker addressing the inequality of the economy.

I had a good sense about him as I researched and followed his path to Newark and the seemingly close bond he had with Pope Francis. After another clergy sexual scandal rocked my faith community, it was clear I needed a new parish. I had checked out one of this prelate's parishes close to where I live. While I had been a member of a parish in the neighboring diocese, I felt a pull toward a new place with someone who took a stand against clergy abuse. Tobin was among the few outspoken advocates of reform, of addressing the harms, those harmed, and holding those clergy of the Church who sexually exploit and violate others responsible, removing them from posts.

As a clerical abuse survivor, I was shaken by the events in

my current parish coupled with the release of the Pennsylvania grand jury report and the revelations concerning retired Cardinal Theodore McCarrick, which hit the front page of the *New York Times* a few months before. A man had come forward, anonymously, sharing with the world that McCarrick had touched him inappropriately when he was a teenager nearly five decades prior. There was further speculation about more abuse by this once revered prince of the Church. An investigation into the abuse of this young boy by McCarrick was found to be credible. At the direction of Pope Francis, McCarrick ceased his public ministry.

As the revelations came to the fore, memories of my own abuse by the pastor swirled in my head. I could relate to the man who came forward, spoke the truth. As with meeting those in AA, there is a bond that exists with others you identify with. Victims feel the pain of other victims.

In previous months I had reached a serene place in my recovery and healing in Christ. But this latest barrage of high-profile news so close to home just threw me. The twins, doubt and despair, always lurking, now raised their ugly heads again.

To speak the truth I had come to, I decided to pen a letter to the *New York Times* after the news broke about McCarrick. The letter was published in the aftermath, expressing my belief that a turning point, long overdue, was happening, especially when members of the hierarchy were directly involved. Among the words I wrote to the editor in response to their June 21 article, "Cardinal Accused of Sexual Abuse Is Removed from Ministry," were these:

I don't buy for one minute that Cardinal Theodore E. McCarrick has absolutely no recollection of sexually abusing a minor 47 years ago.

Coincidentally, it was 47 years ago that I was sexually abused by a Catholic priest. Victims do not forget. I haven't.

Removing a prelate like Cardinal McCarrick so soon after Pope Francis accepted the resignation of Bishop Juan Barros Madrid of Chile, who also claimed loss of memory, feels like a watershed moment.

For the sake of the Church, I hope so.

As I found my seat, and we all settled in, the audience grew quiet. The cardinal was introduced and stepped forward. But before the cardinal began to speak, he closed his eyes, paused in a long silence, and then looked up and scanned the theater. In the silence I could feel his presence. He began:

This evening, I come here with a very heavy heart. When I accepted the opportunity to speak on the economy and all its inequality, especially concerning immigrants, some months ago, the Church—for that matter, the world—hadn't had the Pennsylvania Grand Jury Report or known about the alleged sexual violations by my predecessor, Theodore McCarrick. I don't have the answers, but I do know that the Church must be better, and I ask you for your prayers, patience, and understanding at this very difficult time.

His voice, his words, held sincerity and genuineness. I was grateful that I had come to his talk and heard so much more than the scheduled talk.

Cardinal Tobin continued:

This is a turning point in the Church and only restorative justice can bring us more fully to be disciples in the Joy of the Gospel that our Holy Father, Pope Francis, calls us to be. The truth is that our Lord, Redeemer must guide us, challenge us, heal us, at this very dark moment in the life of the Church, here in the U.S. and across the globe.

Thank you for your profound openness to help and grow from this excruciating pain and adversity. I could not have begun this evening without sharing the hurt I feel, and the entire Church should feel at this hour.

We need to walk together.

Following his talk, I made my way down to the stage area where people were gathered, forming a line to speak to the cardinal. Moved by his candid humility, I felt the need to introduce myself and thank him.

As I approached him, our eyes met, and I reached out my hand.

"Cardinal, my name is Mark Williams, I am a clergy abuse survivor. Thank you for your honesty. I want to offer my help to you—and to be part of the solution."

"Thank you, Mark. I would like that. Let's have coffee soon and talk."

After our brief exchange, I made my way to Broadway to hail a cab, when the cardinal's secretary, Father Jason, caught up with me. "Hi, what is your name again? I heard your conversation with the cardinal."

"Mark Williams."

"Are you the same Mark Williams who wrote the letter in the *New York Times* back in June?"

"Yes."

"We need to meet you, thank you for your voice, the cardinal was quite taken by what you wrote and absolutely agreed."

We arranged to meet around the cardinal's busy schedule. And when I met with Cardinal Tobin in his study at the archdiocesan office across from the Basilica Cathedral of the Sacred Heart in Newark, I shared some of my story which included my journey in recovery. I then told him I was also now nearly fifteen years sober. When I said that, he reached into his pocket and pulled out a familiar AA coin, marking thirty-two years of his own sobriety. And he responded, "I knew there was something about you that I liked right away. There are no coincidences."

From that moment, a friendship was born.

15

Accompaniment and Hope in Francis

The ability to sit down and listen to others, typical of interpersonal encounters, is paradigmatic of the welcoming attitude shown by those who transcend narcissism and accept others, caring for them and welcoming them into their lives. We must not lose our ability to listen. Saint Francis heard the voice of God, he heard the voice of the poor, he heard the voice of the infirm, and he heard the voice of nature. My desire is that the seed that Saint Francis planted may grow in the hearts of many.
—Pope Francis (Encyclical Letter, *Fratelli Tutti*)

Among the conversations with Cardinal Tobin that developed in the following years, I heard him reflect on that summer of 2018, telling me it was the most difficult time of his priesthood. The McCarrick saga blindsided him. McCarrick, he said, was in his backyard. Some of Tobin's fellow bishops had failed miserably, knowing of McCarrick's sexual abuses; they weren't transparent; they turned away, keeping his harmful secret. Tobin was astonished to learn of other prelates whose failure was so strikingly obvious when the Pennsylvania grand jury summary was made public. The summary identified nearly three hundred abusive priests, as well as additional priests and bishops implicated for covering up the abuses of over a thousand victims.

After reviewing the summary, Cardinal Tobin responded. In both deep sadness and anger, he sent out a pastoral letter, published in every church bulletin, to his fellow pilgrims across the Newark Archdiocese, writing:

> We are now realizing that some bishops did not enter into the covenant we call the Charter for the Protection of Children and Young People wholeheartedly. This is sinful and unacceptable. It has caused irreparable harm to every priest's and bishop's relationship with the faithful. Only intentional acts of restorative justice can help us reform and renew a deeply wounded Church.

And so unaware was Cardinal Tobin—or I—at that moment of how much more was to come with the Vatican's own report on the rise and fall of McCarrick, his resignation from the College of Cardinals, and removal from the priesthood, as well as the onrush of even more revelations of abuse becoming known across the global Church in places like Chile, France, Germany, Portugal, Spain, Australia, Canada, Mexico, Peru, Philippines, Scotland, and other locales.

Sexual abuse by priests and bishops and the cover-up by some bishops was not just an East Coast problem. Not just an American problem. Geography played no part on this stage. The dam that broke in Boston two decades prior was breaking all over again, all over the world.

On October 5, 2021, the Independent Commission on Sexual Abuse in the French Catholic Church published its report. The commission concluded that from 1950 to 2020 no fewer than 330,000 minors were victims of sexual abuse by clerics or laypersons within the Church.

The revelations of just how many victims of clergy abuse worldwide suffered felt unending. As Lent began back in 2011 close to home, a second grand jury report disclosed that in the Archdiocese of Philadelphia thirty-seven priests credibly accused of sexual abuse or of inappropriate behavior toward minors remained largely active in some ministerial capacity. A few months earlier, the landmark John Jay report was released, outlining the possible causes (structural, hierarchical, personal) of clergy sexual abuse—a study commissioned by the US Roman Catholic bishops.

Around this same Lenten season, Sean Cardinal O'Malley of Boston led a delegation to Ireland to evaluate the life of the Church there; on his return he proclaimed in so many words that Roman Catholicism will virtually disappear from the rhythm of Irish culture in ten years. As the future president of the Pontifical Commission for the Protection of Minors, under Pope Francis, beginning in March 2014, Cardinal O'Malley witnessed more than the near collapse of the Church in Ireland.

The Catholic Church was once viewed by many as a spiritual bulwark against the world's more destructive tendencies, but that puritanical image of Ireland has changed. The reasons for the decline of the Church are complex, but acknowledged scandals such as historical abuse by priests and nuns was a major factor.
—Michael Kelly, former editor of "Irish Catholic," quoted in the *Belfast Telegraph*

In Ireland and in so many places around the globe we are at a watershed moment in our beloved yet broken Church. People are leaving the pews in numbers that are staggering. The Church cannot sustain itself on its present course. And Roman Catholics will not continue to embrace a hierarchical Church if those appointed to lead us do not promote healing, a healing that includes forgiveness—but not exoneration—for abusive priests and those bishops who acted to cover up the truth. Removing them all from active ministry must be part of a Church moving forward.

Pope Francis, along with his brother bishops throughout the Church, must discern where we go from here, after the grand jury report out of Pennsylvania, and more recently responding to the Attorney General of Maryland Report about the Archdiocese of Baltimore where 600 children and minors were abused by some 150 clerics.

Even more credible reports of cover-ups are emerging in countries around the globe underscored by special independent commissions. They continue to reveal the extent of the history of systemic clerical abuse in the Church. The numbers, the proportions, are staggering.

So many in the Church are hurting: good lay people, good priests, good nuns alike, but no one suffers more than those who have been abused. There is no greater pain than the feeling of shame that victims carry when carrying a shame that is not theirs, put on them as their trust was violated, their bodies were violated.

In view of the roiling events, by February 2019, Pope Francis held a landmark conference in Rome on the scandal. Just a few months prior, at the US Bishops' annual plenary session in Baltimore, the bishops discussed McCarrick, the grand jury report, and the troubling related matters facing the Church not only in the United States but beyond its shores. One of their own, a man highly touted throughout the greater Church, a gifted fundraiser, worldly, charming, trusted advisor to popes, had abused so many, had covered it up for so long, had caused irreparable harm.

What's been revealed over the last decades, close to home and far from home, is that clerical sexual abuse is global. The "universal church," which should have been attending the broken, has been revealed as the broken one, requiring the field hospital that Pope Francis called for. The Church has seen the breaking, the marginalization of those it has portended to help. But it is those who are abused who must now be centered in order for the Church to heal. The Church ought to help the troubled men too—the predators—but never at the expense of the faithful.

In the spirit of accompaniment, in November 2022, I accepted an invitation by the United States Conference of Catholic Bishops (USCCB) to offer a reflection alongside Cardinal Joseph Tobin. Our talks to the entire assembly of the American bishops and various gathered staff members coincided with the twentieth anniversary of "The Charter for the Protection of Children and Young People," commonly known as the "Dallas Charter," enacted originally in 2002 by the bishops to establish comprehensive procedures and offer guidelines for reconciliation, healing, accountability, and prevention of future acts of abuse.

Beyond any doubt, the hands of the bishops were forced by the *Boston Globe*'s Spotlight team of investigative journalists who uncovered an extensive horrific history of sexual abuse of children and minors by Catholic priests—as well as a calculated cover-up of the abuse by the hierarchy in the Archdiocese of Boston and beyond.

And now, in this Synod on Synodality time, the charter is being revised yet again by the bishops and expert associates, following previous revisions in 2005, 2011, and 2018. Increasing challenges in the life of the Church both in the United States and across the global Church with respect to the sexual abuse scandal demands up-to-date best practices to ensure that all the people of the Church are protected and as needed given every opportunity, support, and resource to be healed.

The synod on synodality is a time for listening to one another throughout the entire Church, especially the marginalized, in order to imagine a different Church, a more vibrant and caring institution that reaches all brothers and sisters more deeply. I believe victims of abuse must be heard in order to bring lasting healing at this hour in the life of the Church. Among the things I said to the gathered bishops at the USCCB plenary meeting on November 15, 2022, were these:

> The countless abused in our midst desire to walk with you. We hunger for communion, to come together and partake of the bread of life, to share the Eucharist, to have Christ's body and blood heal us. I believe the Church is the solution, the way back and the way forward. It is the shared suffering of Calvary. It is the peace of reconciliation found in the living presence of the risen Lord. That peace fills one's core when healing comes after the deep shame felt, the piercing pain of sexual abuse, a pain compounded by those who do not listen to the voices of victims.
>
> . . . Synodality calls upon us to be open to the relationships that heal, that truly help, that engender faith. The synodal way, the common path, our shared road of the "Good News" is not an abstract idea. Rather, its fruit is realized through grace, especially out of suffering. *Hope is real. Hope is Christ. Hope is found walking together.* Those hurt in the Church and by the Church must be part of the transformative grace that is the cross.

Tomorrow I fly to the eternal city to be with my Global Collaborative colleagues, and fellow survivors: Dr. Jennifer Wortham, Archdiocese of Boston; Michael Hoffman, Archdiocese of Chicago, affirmed by Cardinal Blasé Cupich; Fr. Jerry McGlone, Archdiocese of Washington; and many others to join other survivors near and far and leaders who work on behalf of victims and survivors from around the globe, especially our trusted brother and friend, Fr. Hans Zollner in Rome—with great comfort in our Holy Father's blessing—to celebrate this year, November 18 and every year thereafter—as commissioned by the United Nations: *The World Day for the Prevention of, and Healing from, Child Sexual Exploitation, Abuse and Violence.*

This remarkable event would not have been possible without you, the American bishops. . . . Your collective voice to make the Charter part of the DNA of our Church in 2002—two decades ago led by Bishop—now Cardinal— Wilton Gregory—was necessary and prophetic.

As our Holy Father has shared, "The Synod on Synodality is not to create another Church, but to create a different Church."

After I spoke, Cardinal Tobin then addressed the USCCB General Assembly, with a mixture of pastoral exhortation, humility, and his description of accompanying those—deeply listening to those—whose lives have been scarred and devastated. Among his words were these:

> The act of providing emotional, physical, and spiritual support to people in need as well as walking in their shoes is a critical part in recognizing the human dignity and experience of every person. In his first apostolic exhortation, *The Joy of the Gospel*—arguably the programmatic statement of his pontificate—he teaches that the Church will have to initiate everyone—priests, religious, and laity—into this

"art of accompaniment" which teaches us to remove our sandals before the sacred ground of the other (cf. Ex 3:5) (*Evangelii Gaudium*, 169).

Accompanying victims of sexual abuse always demands humility, especially when the abuse has been perpetrated by clerics. . . . At times a meeting with a victim means sitting silent before a torrent of accusations, insults, and gut-wrenching screams. To my knowledge, in the accounts of healing preserved in the Gospels, no one comes to Jesus with a sanguine request to "feel better."

Listening to the Word of God, I hear shrieks of pain as a person names the torment and the tormentor. There have been meetings that showed me that I personally could do nothing for the person who just left my office. My hope is that, in naming the source of their suffering to a representative of those who caused it, an obstacle might be cleared that had prevented the healing grace of Jesus from reaching them in all its abundance. That the more our Church was perceived as a field hospital, the better the chance that another disciple would be an instrument of God's grace. . . .

. . . The eyes of both disciples were eventually opened by Jesus on the walk to Emmaus. As this Assembly marks a milestone in our pilgrimage—the 20th anniversary of the Dallas Charter and the *Essential Norms*—let us continue to listen to the cries of victims and survivors—*walk with them*—so that our eyes may be opened, and the abundant gifts entrusted to the Church are accessible to all.

Later that week, following the USCCB meeting, I went to Rome, where I had a providential encounter with Pope Francis and the opportunity to personally thank him for his care of sexual abuse victims in our Church as well as his support of the

UN World Day. To those of us who gathered, I was struck by how gentle and kind he was to our small gathered number of women and men, survivors from around the world. I gave him copies of my and Cardinal Tobin's talks to his brother bishops in the United States, along with a handwritten note. Before we left him, he asked those in our group to pray for him. And he said he would pray for us.

Struck by the graced set of moments with our group and our exchange with the pope, as I was later walking in St. Peter's Square reflecting on the meeting, I said to myself, "There is a God." This is something I recalled my friend Brian relating to me after he met with Bishop Scicluna in Scotland, a decade ago. As the bishop walked out of Brian's house, he looked back at him and called out, "There is a God."

Several months after the trip, I received a letter from Monsignor Roberto Campisi at the Vatican:

Dear Mr. Williams,

I am writing to acknowledge the note that you sent to His Holiness Pope Francis, together with your presentation to the Bishops of the United States during their Plenary Assembly.

His Holiness has read the documentation and is most grateful for your continuing efforts with regard to the protection of children and young people. He trusts that your work will serve to foster healing, reconciliation and peace within the Church.

The Way of the Cross
and the Eucharist

Amen, amen I say to you, whoever believes in me will do the works that I do, and will do greater ones than these, because I am going to the Father. And whatever you ask in my name, I will do, so that the Father may be glorified in the Son. If you ask anything of me in my name, I will do it.

—John 14:12–14

The cross and the Eucharist have been the twin lifelines of my healing. Although the Church may have abandoned many of us who have been victims of abuse, God never has. The difficult road I walk, I do not walk alone.

That paradox of finding healing within the sacraments of the Church has led me to understand that my healing would not have been possible without truth-telling and without the Church. While many are retraumatized by the Church and are not able for multiple reasons to return, I have felt called, step by step, toward addressing the current crisis of the Church *within the Church itself,* and to advocate for a Church where victims/

survivors play a leading role in the transformative healing necessary to make the Church not only different from its past, but a
better, safer place of merciful love that touches all.

My friend, colleague, and fellow survivor Jennifer Wortham
included her 2016 letter to Pope Francis in her book *A Letter
to the Pope*. She wrote the letter before meeting with the pope
in Rome.

Part of what she wrote in the letter speaks to the redemption
we seek:

> The Church is an institution. Institutions are merely a
> collection of people. All people are sinners, and while the
> cloth does not protect one from evil, we must recognize that
> those who wear the cloth are but servants of God, sinners
> on a path to enlightenment, as we all are. Christ's legacy
> of forgiveness, peace, hope, and everlasting salvation must
> endure. If we do not open our hearts and forgive all those
> who have transgressed against us, we will never experience
> the joy of grace.

The journey really never ends. The Cross is still the life, the
soul, and the love of becoming whole. My journey is just beginning. I needed those years of sobriety, reflection, and a deepening
faith to find healing and to step toward being a voice for others
harmed by the Church. I also needed Jorge Bergoglio—now
Pope Francis—to change his own heart, in order to become a
friend to and advocate for victims across the world.

For our brothers and sisters, especially those whose poverty
of spirit isolates and crushes them due to abuse by clergy, the
call of each of us, the call on the Church is to do what we can to
console, support, love, and provide resources. Pope Francis urges
us to *go out to the field hospital and help the wounded.*

For me, the road of freedom has been God's loving grace. My ultimate spiritual director, the Holy Spirit. And the gift of so much of that loving grace has been witnessed through those who accompanied me along the road of broken things. My wife, Karen, and our family first and foremost. In their love I grow in love. Our love is stronger than ever as time passes and as I've been honest with them about what I went through all those years ago. God's loving grace has also included my AA mentors who asked the most important questions. And includes those doctors who worked with me and those priests, bishops, advocates, and friends such as Cardinal Tobin—who seek a true, healing Church, one that is restored, one that protects the most vulnerable among us, one that forgives *and* holds accountable those individuals who have harmed, sexually exploited the vulnerable and also by doing so have harmed the whole Church. We all work together on this in our flawed and holy ways. I have been blessed by the bonds of those who have extended and shared God's loving grace.

But the others who have shared the healing path of the cross in their stories, words, and voices have been the fellow survivors of abuse in the Catholic Church. From them I have heard and shared stories harrowing, courageous, moving, and uplifting. As we together struggle to hold on to faith, a higher power, a healing path, we have sought to tame the demons of trauma.

Last Lent, I had the very moving experience of participating in the "Way of the Cross Prayer Service," held by Awake—a community of abuse survivors, concerned Catholics, and allies committed to awakening, transformation, and healing from the wounds of sexual abuse in the Catholic Church. The opportunity to participate in this powerful prayer service was a gift from the Awake community to me, and all of us who took part. In our shared Lenten pilgrimage, it was a remarkable opportunity to pray with and for other abuse survivors as we connected our own experiences to the suffering of Jesus Christ in his final days.

The prayer followed the traditional Stations of the Cross devotion, with each station featuring a personal reflection written by an individual who experienced sexual abuse by a Catholic leader. The Awake team added one final station to the number: Station 15, the Resurrection. They did so as many abuse survivors struggle to maintain hope. It was at this station that I read aloud my prayer for the work that has been done and the work of the upcoming 2024 Synod on Synodality, that those who gathered would imagine a different Church at this moment in the twenty-first century, would somehow take in these voices of their fellow Catholics who have suffered abuse in the Church. We have shared the Paschal Mystery deeply. We have touched the Cross, and our desire is to feel the love of the Risen One from outside our tombs, as well, Arisen.

One by one we told our stories, reflected, and prayed. And shared our suffering, the suffering of survivors, beside each station of the cross, with the one who suffered with us, alongside us, for us.

Leader: The First Station— Jesus Is Condemned to Death

Reader 1: A reflection from Michael—"Jesus, you stood alone before Pilate, like I stood alone before the priest. Nobody was there to speak up for you, or me. Nobody defended you, or me. Even more than fifty years after my abuse began, sometimes I feel alone, abandoned, or afraid. Sometimes I feel like I have been condemned to a journey of recurring images of the suffering I endured. Other victims I knew were so condemned to mental anguish that it led to their deaths, and for them I weep. But because of your passion and death, I also know you walk with me, and all survivors, in our journey toward wholeness and redemption. Thank you for the grounding of this truth in my life."

Leader: For all victims, survivors, thrivers, and copers, let us pray: Jesus, hear us.

All respond: Jesus, be with us.

Leader: The Second Station— Jesus Takes Up His Cross

Reader 2: A reflection from Jessica—"Acknowledging and facing the abuse I had suffered in childhood felt like an insurmountable task, one that needed to be dealt with so I could 'get on' with the life you were calling me to. Looking into your eyes as you accepted the cross, hours after praying for this cup to pass you by, I slowly began to understand that this was a portion of my way of the cross. I continue to learn, when I don't know how to shoulder this burden, that you show me the way. This path isn't unknown to you—you know it well. And your courage calls me to walk next to you."

Leader: For all victims, survivors, thrivers, and copers, let us pray: Jesus, hear us.

All respond: Jesus, be with us.

Leader: The Third Station— Jesus Falls the First Time

Reader 1: A reflection from Cathy—"Lord Jesus, as you walked that road to Calvary, the weight of the cross bore down until it became too much, and you stumbled. Under the weight and burden of my sexual abuse, I too have fallen. I fell as you fell. As I looked down at the dirt-covered ground, I felt shame, disappointment, and fear. I felt so very alone on that early part of my journey. I have struggled, but, through you, Lord, have been able to get back on my feet. As I move forward with uncertain steps, I can say with confidence that the abuse was not my fault. I know this road will not be easy, but it is possible with you. Be with me, Lord."

Leader: For all victims, survivors, thrivers, and copers, let us pray: Jesus, hear us.

All respond: Jesus, be with us.

Leader: The Fourth Station— Jesus Meets His Mother

Reader 2: A reflection from Phillip—"I think about the pain you were suffering and the pain you knew was to come, then the experience of meeting your mother in the middle of it all. After the first time I was abused as a young child, I was picked up by my mom to go back home. I was crying and did not say anything. She was not able to comfort me as she did not know about the abuse I had just suffered. Still, just being next to her was finally a safe place for me. It makes me think about how this short time with your Mother must have been a very bittersweet but still encouraging encounter."

Leader: For all victims, survivors, thrivers, and copers, let us pray: Jesus, hear us.

All respond: Jesus, be with us.

Leader: The Fifth Station— Simon of Cyrene Helps Jesus Carry His Cross

Reader 1: A reflection from Wendy—"I was terrified to speak of the sexual abuse I endured for three years from my spiritual director. I felt that what I had to share would be a burden too difficult for others to carry. I had carried this burden alone for forty years and thought it in the best interest of my closest family members and friends to keep it to myself and spare them the crushing pain that had plagued me for so many decades. I hadn't realized how heavy this cross was until parts of it were lifted off my heart. I was overwhelmed with humility and gratitude once I began to speak, as friends and family held me, cried with and for me and have continued to support me with tenderness and careful attention. I wonder if you felt the same way when Simon lifted the burden of the cross off your body.

You didn't stop Simon and inform him that the cross would be too much. You didn't assume others couldn't handle it. You allowed Simon to share in the pain, which must have made the weight more bearable."

Leader: For all victims, survivors, thrivers, and copers, let us pray: Jesus, hear us.

All respond: Jesus, be with us.

Leader: The Sixth Station— Veronica Wipes the Face of Jesus

Reader 2: A reflection from Carol—"Abused as a child, and growing up with parents who were unaware or could not face the reality of my abuse, I learned to hide my shame, to hide my face from the world around me. I rarely made eye contact, and I avoided painful places and memories. On my journey of healing, you have placed Veronicas in my life who haven't turned away from the ugliness of my story, who have been willing to look at my face, offer a spiritual cloth, and listen with kindness, interest and empathy—the comfort needed to help me continue to carry the cross of surrender."

Leader: For all victims, survivors, thrivers, and copers, let us pray: Jesus, hear us.

All respond: Jesus, be with us.

Leader: The Seventh Station— Jesus Falls the Second Time

Reader 1: A reflection from Mike—"The clergy abuse I endured as a child caused me to feel isolated, with no one to turn to. I didn't have anyone to lighten my burden, lift me up, or encourage me to go on. Now as an adult, I have a support system: my family, friends, good priests, and many others who can lift me up when I fall. As I continue to carry my own cross of childhood trauma, I have experienced tender and sweet heartfelt connections from others, who have comforted me and calmed my anxieties. These people help me to be resilient in the face of painful triggers. Any connection, like lifting someone up when they fall a second time, can provide comfort and make a difference."

Leader: For all victims, survivors, thrivers, and copers, let us pray: Jesus, hear us.

All respond: Jesus, be with us.

Leader: The Eighth Station— Jesus Meets the Women of Jerusalem

Reader 2: A reflection from Emily—"Sometimes I can't weep for you. So often your passion is portrayed as taking away our suffering, or worse, as trumping our suffering so we have no room to complain. Are you hurt that I can't find consolation in your wounds because mine still run so deep, that your three days of passion sound mercifully short to me in the five years since my abuse? But you see the weeping of the women no one else sees. And you say, 'Daughters of Jerusalem, do not weep for me, but weep for yourselves and for your children.' Your grief for the suffering of women and children is an acknowledgment of my suffering, your invitation for me to weep for me rather than for you. You've made my suffering, my sexual assault, part of your passion. You invite my passion to become a part of your passion on the way to your own cross. You stand in your passion and invite me to weep for mine. I suppose I can weep for that, after all."

Leader: For all victims, survivors, thrivers, and copers, let us pray: Jesus, hear us.

All respond: Jesus, be with us.

Leader: The Ninth Station— Jesus Falls the Third Time

Reader 1: A reflection from Megan—"There is no escaping the weight of this cross, but I start to feel like I can manage in my weakness. I picture the abuse as the first fall, the reporting and the immense pain that it brought as the second. You've given me Veronicas, your Mother, and Simons along the way. But then this third fall comes, on any random Sunday morning when I just can't take one more step into that Church. Or I get the courage to go inside and there my abuser is. Or the readings of the day are the same ones he used to groom me. I feel so exposed. Weak. Alone. I wonder if people are shocked any more when You fall this third time. When I continue to fall and I can't move, do the people [abusers] who gave the cross even see [us] anymore? Or have they all turned away? Is there any more scandal at how heavy [this cross] already is? Thank you, Jesus, for not leaving me alone down here in the dust."

Leader: For all victims, survivors, thrivers, and copers, let us pray: Jesus, hear us.

All respond: Jesus, be with us.

Leader: The Tenth Station— Jesus Is Stripped of His Garments

Reader 2: A reflection from Natalie—"When I disclose my abuse to a new person, I feel myself stripped naked, my emotional wounds ripped open with each fresh telling of this terrible story. So many feelings come rushing back, as strongly as they did when I first told someone: the fear that I will be ignored, the pain from previous dismissals by ministers and mentors and colleagues, the lie of shame that I somehow asked for it or deserved it. Though I remain dedicated to sharing my story, I am always ready to be ridiculed, challenged unfairly, or called a liar for the truths that I tell. The exposure is paralyzing in those moments as I wait for their response, praying that I will not be met with mockery again."

Leader: For all victims, survivors, thrivers, and copers, let us pray: Jesus, hear us.

All respond: Jesus, be with us.

Leader: The Eleventh Station— Jesus Is Nailed to the Cross

Reader 1: A reflection from Jennifer—"Jesus, as the nails were driven through your flesh to affix you to the cross, my abuser also drove nails through my soul that affixed me to this cross on which he callously left me to hang. The agony of the three hours you hung there, the humiliation of being nailed to the cross, so exposed as onlookers watched and jeered—I've felt this too, as a woman abused as an adult, the humiliation as onlookers to my abuse jeered and gossiped. Oh, the agony. . . . Jesus, I've never known a pain as intense as the aftermath of what that priest did to me. When you asked your Father, 'Forgive them, for they know not what they do,' it makes it easier for me to forgive those who had no idea the gravity of the abuse I endured. As you accepted being nailed to your cross, I look to you to help me accept being nailed to mine and trust that you will use it for your glory."

Leader: For all victims, survivors, thrivers, and copers, let us pray: Jesus, hear us.

All respond: Jesus, be with us.

Leader: The Twelfth Station— Jesus Dies on the Cross

Reader 2: A reflection from Esther—"Seeing the abuse crisis continue to ravage the Body of Christ brings me a hopelessness that is overwhelming. Seeing the pain of other victim/survivors pierces my heart with pain. Despair then creeps in as I battle my memories, my shame, and the apathetic attitude of many Church leaders. Jesus, after having to endure such cruelty and shame, your last words spoke of the trust you had in the Father. All hope seemed lost as you bowed your head and died. Despair grips my heart, but in that darkness came the greatest victory. By the power of your death and resurrection, may we find renewed hope and trust in God's loving mercy and justice."

Leader: For all victims, survivors, thrivers, and copers, let us pray: Jesus, hear us.

All respond: Jesus, be with us.

Leader: The Thirteenth Station— Jesus Is Taken Down from the Cross

Reader 1: A reflection from Gigi—"At this station, my heart remembers those that treated me with tender loving care as I was taken down from my own cross—both the abuse I endured and the horror of the reporting process. I remember a colleague who held me when I had a nervous breakdown at work. And a friend who prayed over me after I reported my abuser.

And a loved one who courageously asked me if I was going to hurt myself and said she would be sad if I wasn't here anymore. Thank you, Lord, for the amazing people in my life who gave me hope when I did not want to live anymore. Thank you for reminding me of your providence in this difficult time and that good people do exist."

Leader: For all victims, survivors, thrivers, and copers, let us pray: Jesus, hear us.

All respond: Jesus, be with us.

Leader: The Fourteenth Station— Jesus Is Laid in the Tomb

Reader 2: A reflection from Lisa—"After the reality of my abuse set in, I often wondered if I would ever be able to find Jesus again. For years, my soul had been invaded and the person of Jesus was confounded with my abuser. Prayer became, and sometimes still is, a time of frustration and fear where I cannot separate them. But here in the tomb, I find hope. Here in the tomb, the stone is rolled shut and you are there, Jesus. Only you. There is no one else except you and me. Here in the tomb I have hope that our relationship will one day be whole again."

Leader: For all victims, survivors, thrivers, and copers, let us pray: Jesus, hear us.

All respond: Jesus, be with us.

Leader: The Fifteenth Station— Jesus Is Raised from the Dead

Reader 1: A reflection from Mark—"There are times when I am overcome by the darkness of the tomb, by the raw wood of the cross, raw against my rawness from being abused. But my shame and wounds are healed by you, the Risen One, who suffered, died, and rose for all, especially the sexually exploited and violated. Lord, your paschal journey is our paschal journey. We can heal and we can rise in the joy that is Easter. Like the women at the tomb that early morning, let us be open to that same vision of angels announcing that you are alive. Let us hold onto our own lives in your love—in gratitude that we too are alive.

Leader: For all victims, survivors, thrivers, and copers, let us pray: Jesus, hear us.

All respond: Jesus, be with us.

Concluding Prayer to Way of the Cross Prayer Service

God of love, you hear the cries of all who have been wounded by abuse in the Catholic Church. Grant them your healing, justice, and peace.

Jesus, gentle companion, you accompany those who suffer. May all who are hurting know your merciful presence in their lives.

Holy Spirit, mighty advocate, you stir within us and awaken our hearts. Help us to see where you are leading us today and give us the strength to say yes to your call.

Amen.

17

Walking the Synodal Road: Journeying Together toward Healing

So humble yourselves under the mighty hand of God, that he may exalt you in due time. Cast all your worries upon him because he cares for you. Be sober and vigilant. Your opponent the devil is prowling around like a roaring lion looking for [someone] to devour. Resist him, steadfast in faith, knowing that your fellow believers throughout the world undergo the same sufferings. The God of all grace who called you to his eternal glory through Christ [Jesus] will himself restore, confirm, strengthen, and establish you after you have suffered a little. To him be dominion forever. Amen.

—1 Peter 5:6–11

In AA, as I've mentioned, it's often said that "we are as sick as our secrets." That same holds for the Church. Those who speak the truth of the harmful secrets of the Church are those who form a scaffolding for a future restored Church.

I have witnessed in my own journey the ways Church leaders

such as Cardinal Tobin have accompanied me and others in the stations of the cross we observe. I have listened as he has called out some of his fellow bishops for failing to do more to stem the tide of abusive behavior within the Church. Change demands truth, and truth demands the abolition of secrets.

To me, this is where the work of restorative justice begins. Restorative justice answer two fundamental questions:

1. How does the Church come clean?
2. How do victims of clerical sexual abuse feel whole again?

Restorative justice will be fully realized within the Church, for those in and out of the pews, if the Church in full transparency tells the truth about all the harms perpetrated by priests, religious, and lay members of the Church who have created this sexual abuse crisis. Those who have been abused by Catholic clergy, religious, and lay persons who work in the Church deserve nothing less. The truth must be spoken, so the truth can set us free. This is the work of restorative justice.

In her book *God's Tender Mercy: Reflections on Forgiveness*, Sr. Joan Chittister, Benedictine churchwoman and author, wrote:

Weeping is a very life-giving thing. It wizens the soul of the individual and it sounds alarms in society. The book of Ecclesiastes may be nowhere more correct than here. There is definitely a time for weeping. If we do not weep on a personal level, we shall never understand other human beings.

There is no greater time, no deeper need, in the history of the Church to weep. We must hear the cries of the wounded, the sexually abused in our midst.

The abused have been profoundly hurt in the Church. Their cross, my cross, has been hard, at times unbearably heavy, but as I experienced the shared weight of the cross in those fifteen stations together with those who understood my pain, I knew I needed to carry that weight, and to share that weight, and to speak of that weight in order to grow more fully in the one crucified.

Predators and victims alike share in this journey of the cross—the radical *Christus* that lives within each soul, in all our brokenness and sin, absorbs into his divine, human self the sins of all who call on him, all he calls his own.

In the years to come, "Forgive us our trespasses as we forgive those who trespass against us" must not mean perpetuating the ongoing secrecy nor avoiding accountability. We must speak of what needs forgiveness. What it means is owning up to the truth. To understand the gospel, we must live the good news of the truth that sets us free.

Only by forgiving my abuser did I find inner peace. But I have not forgotten. And I never will. In the words of Carl Jung: "*I am not what happened to me. I am what I choose to become.*"

> I believe true restorative justice is not about punishment; rather it must be centered on the fruits of healing by all involved, especially those harmed. Perpetrators must be held to account, but if they are forgiven, however hard, interior freedom will come in time. I consider the healing work of restorative justice as, in part, the work of forgiveness—not exoneration.

Nearly fifty years removed from my abuse, I realize I needed to hit rock bottom to face the darkness, to speak the truth, to find and feel God's light. Sober, naked to the truth, I have found in the Eucharist the path to an authentic life. The journey of healing never really ends. For any of us. Yes, for me, the cross has been my life, my soul, my love, and my becoming whole through Christ's wholeness.

When we fall, we must be open to heal, to embrace our brokenness. Station by station of our pain, of our walking with Jesus on the way of the cross, we become weavers of a restorative justice fabric sewn with mercy and unwavering compassion of our stories with God.

~

A month after Pope Francis had convened the international gathering of Church officials to address the clerical abuse scandal, I learned that the primary organizer, Rev. Hans Zollner, SJ, a Jesuit from Bavaria, trained psychotherapist, former seminary professor, and one of the founding members of the Pontifical Commission for the Protection of Minors, had been among those who read my *New York Times* letter to the editor about my having been abused at the hands of a priest, where I wrote among other things, these words:

> Truth didn't seem to matter. Clericalism ruled. Secrets abounded. Files were concealed. Grand juries were never part of the lexicon. But victims never forget. The pope should encourage healing and offer forgiveness—however contrarian this sounds—but he cannot exonerate his brother priests who committed and covered up this sin. The defrocking last week of Theodore McCarrick, the former cardinal and archbishop of Washington who was found guilty by the Church of sexual abuse, sent a hopeful message before the summit. His removal was so right. More must follow.

Soon after I wrote that letter to the editor, two friends associated with the Center on Religion and Culture at Fordham University contacted me. David and Maureen both shared that Hans Zollner was coming to New York City to give a talk and that he wanted to meet me after reading my *New York Times* piece.

After his talk I sat down with Fr. Zollner in a nearby room, and he told me that in reading my letter to the editor, he was inspired by the clarity and the call for change. He then asked me: "After being abused by a priest, where does your faith come from?"

"From Jesus Christ and his cross. All of us face suffering and I have suffered, but I feel free in his resurrection, in finding my voice in and by his truth."

"I find," Fr. Hans said, "many victims become retraumatized when they come into contact with priests again, even though these men are not abusers; how do you overcome this?"

"I believe inner peace comes with forgiveness, certainly not by forgetting, always holding those who abused and covered up to account. But without forgiving those who hurt us, the priest who hurt me, I myself could not be free. This road has provided the fruits found in the twenty-third Psalm, that *surely goodness and mercy shall follow me all the days of my life.* I pray this comes true for all victims."

"Mark," he said, looking at me, "will you help me and our Church to heal?"

While I always understood AA as being part of a path of healing and the beginning of support for others in their journey, and I considered how that might also be important in supporting others harmed by clergy abuse, I can't say there was a sense of calling that was pronounced, only after I responded to conversations, invitations, the nudgings of the Holy Spirit step by step did I realize, as with Fr. Zollner's invitation, that something was forming a calling, if I would but respond. There and then the work expanded, and a friendship was formed.

I thought back to my friend's calling me an instrument for the healing of others, for change. I don't know exactly what that means, but I am seeking to continue to live in grace and freedom, accepting the abundance of my friend's words as a confirmation of a call to be part of the solution during this truly historic time in the life of the Church, as Father Hans, Pope Francis's globetrotting voice of healing on the clerical abuse scandal, has called it.

18

Forgiveness,
not Exoneration

*Yet even now, says the Lord, return to me with your
whole heart, with fasting, and weeping, and mourning;
Rend your hearts, not your garments and return to the
Lord, your God. For gracious and merciful is he, slow
to anger, rich in kindness, and relenting in punishment.*
—Joel 2:12–13

In wintertime of 2011 I took a step a long time in the making:
I went to the grave of my abuser. The glossy green pines, wind-
swept and gently snow-covered, greeted me one by one, left and
right, as I drove under their arch into the cemetery toward the
Vermont marble altar sitting firmly in the center of the grass
turnaround. I was halfway into the cemetery and couldn't help
but notice how many more headstones covered the landscape
since my last visit.

For a moment, I paused to remember both my parents'
funerals and their burials here. The draped American flag over
my father's coffin. The faces looking down at the empty dirt
hole awaiting my mother's casket. This resting place that had
doubled in size.

The newer graves did not reflect the mature surroundings around the old tombstones where pink and white azaleas, Japanese dogwoods, winterberry holly, boxwood shrubs, and native fescue formed a collage of nature's radiance. Yet the beauty remained, and all of it was peaceful to my bones. I rolled down my window as I approached the place to park.

The ocean was near. Salt filled the air. Canada geese honked above, flying in a free-flowing triangle toward the bay. Faded Christmas poinsettias surrounded me like fallen soldiers, their spindly stems and brittle leaves reaching out over the dusty snow.

I parked, got out, and stood leaning on the hood. Standing there, I glanced north at endless gray stones and noticed many white crosses. I recognized two massively lavish tombs and was struck again by the beauty of one sculpture in the distance, bronze, modern, almost five feet tall, the crucified Christ.

In the silence, I whispered, "God, who are these dead beneath me? What were their lives like? Who came to visit them? Did they have a family? Friends? Where are they now? Heaven? Is there such a place?" Surely there is.

This can't be the end. "Do you hear me, God?" I said. "Does anyone hear me right now? Please, God, *don't* abandon me now. Please."

Suddenly, a single pheasant flew past me, climbing quickly, brilliant feathers against the sky, its tail long and beak erect; its flight strong. I stood silently. In the chill of this February morning, I was alone, and it was time to take that step.

First, I walked to my parents' resting place. They were buried twenty-three years apart next to the grave of the father of my childhood friend Timothy, who was killed by a motorist just after our Holy Communion in May 1964. When I visited the cemetery, I always thought of my First Eucharist and how Karl Rahner, SJ, captured what it meant in *The Eucharist: The Mystery of Our Christ*:

And thus He says: "Take this Body, which is given for you, drink this blood poured out for you." And through the power of His creative word which changes the subsoils of reality, He makes Himself exist in the form of bread and wine, the everyday sign of loving unity with his disciples, so that all of this—His sacrificed reality for their salvation—becomes manifest and manifestly operative; it truly belongs to them and enters into the center of their being. "Take, eat, this is my body; Drink . . . for this is my blood of the new covenant which is poured out for you." They take and they are taken. Taken by the redeeming power of obedience and the love of the Lord, taken by His death which gives birth out of its dreadful void, encircled by the grace of God which, with the incomprehensible and consuming Holiness of God, unites.

On this day, all these years later, the Eucharist was alive in me. Earlier that morning, I had gone to the closed AA meeting that I liked attending when visiting the neighborhood I grew up in. There, a woman reflected on the Seventh Step, sharing softly:

Pain certainly is the price of admission into a new life; it does bring humility, and humility heals the pain. It had healed the excruciating pain I had. I felt such deep pain after my mother's suicide, of her leaving me. I had to let her go. I could no longer drink. I had to find sobriety to find her, to forgive her, to forgive myself, yes, the price of admission to a new way of living, a new life.

I identified with this moving story of her life and loss. I had known that if I could fear the pain less, and somehow rid myself of what haunted me, and desire humility more completely, as written in the Seventh Step of AA, then maybe I could find a greater peace.

What would it mean to truly desire this humility? I had to learn this, feel this, embrace this, live this, even love this, humbly walking with my creator, my God, asking him to remove my shortcomings.

I continued to listen to others share for the rest of the hour in that church basement, and I shut my eyes just before the meeting's end. Within myself, I whispered over and over what Father Richard Rohr has encouraged us to say in prayer: "Turn your wounds into sacred gifts. Turn your wounds into sacred gifts. Turn your wounds into sacred gifts."

The meeting was coming to a close. I opened my eyes, joined hands with the older man to my right and the young woman to my left. All the forty-plus people in the room formed a circle and held hands and recited the serenity prayer in unison: "God, grant me the serenity to accept the things I cannot change, the courage to change the things I can, and the wisdom to know the difference."

Now, I brought all my prayer and my sense of my wounds as sacred gifts to this place. At my parents' grave, light snow covered the beige rock above them.

My father: Joseph R. Williams 1928–1968; my mother: Gwendolyn V. Williams 1930–1991. I brushed the snow off the plaque bolted to the stone. The black letters etched into the square copper plate were weather-beaten, faded, but still readable, that timeless quote my sister and I had chosen:

> *The world without storms and our lives without agony would give us nothing to grow on. Make us glad for stormy weather.*
> —Thomas Merton

Merton's words remained pure, precise, real, raw. Pain was the price of admission. We grow from agony. "Yes, turn your wounds into sacred gifts," I said faintly, as I made the sign of the cross and spoke to my parents, "I love you."

I then walked around a few grave sites across the cobblestone drive toward the marble altar. The pastor who abused me was buried there, next to his successor. Today would have been his hundredth birthday; he'd been dead eleven years. *The courage to change the things I can.*

I knelt in the snow in front of his gravestone. It was a simple, flat, shiny black and green block, lying just above the surface. His name was carved into it, and the dates of his birth and death, the years he had served the parish were marked at its base. The altar looked like it was coming out of the ground, as I lifted my head and shoulders, my hands covering my kneecaps.

Through tears that came and came and came, I spoke aloud, "I do not understand why you touched me the way you did. I do not understand many things. I was just a boy. I know you were a man of faith. You taught me much, despite the times—well, you know what I mean," I said, naming and not naming the abuse. Naming and not naming the confusion of feeling cared for and being violated. But he did know. "On this birthday, this hundredth anniversary of your birth, you deserve my forgiveness. I need to forgive you. I must forgive myself. It was so long ago. I have to have serenity. You can understand this, can't you? Will you? God does. I know this now. I must go."

I stood up, and before I walked back to my car, I opened my palms and spread out my arms, looked down at his grave and through my tears spoke again to him:

"I must have peace, and I must let it go. I must keep my sobriety. I forgive you. And I do know my God is with me now. I didn't back then. When I'm lost, God is with me. He has entered my brokenness and is making me whole. I needed to tell you this: I'm alive, I'm well, and I'm on the right road. I've been transformed and can go on. I have no doubt God is with you too. I know He forgives you. I forgive you."

To truly live in this world, to realize the fullness of our lives, we must start to break the silences of wrong. As Martin Luther King Jr. preached: "*Our lives begin to end the day we become silent about things that matter.*"

My own abuser passed a long time ago, but that day when I knelt at his grave, I still had to ask why. I had no other choice; I told him he was wrong. But for me to be free, to find the indwelling Christ, forgiveness needed to be on my lips.

Today, despite my experience, the real Church, the living faith community, the cross and the Eucharist have never been closer to me. Through the community of those who suffered abuse speaking their pain and also through friends and spiritual mentors with me on the path of speaking the truth and holding perpetrators to account and seeking restorative justice—Pope Francis, Cardinal Tobin, Fr. Hans—and many other good priests and lay friends of faith, I have been shown that the Church is not buildings or priests or structures, it is truly the mystical body of Christ. It is Christ's flesh.

Over time, my life has been restored through God's grace and my active acceptance of that grace. It's an acceptance that I see in some of the steps and words of AA:

> *Step 2: Came to believe that a Power greater than ourselves could restore us to sanity.*
> *Step 3: Made a decision to turn our will and our lives over to the care of God as we understood him.*

These steps have played an enormous part in my own healing. Grace was with me to take action and free myself from a destructive and self-serving ego. Grace was with me when I had to remove the drink to see just how much abuse shaped my distorted views.

Healing comes when we realize that God is there to help, that others are there to help, that we no longer need to be afraid nor stay wedded to alcoholism. To enjoy what it means to be clean and sober offered me the opportunity to know myself, to be present and ready for whatever life throws at me. In that grace, clarity of voice, mind, heart, spirit, and soul makes for a good day, always.

I am a witness to how those abused as children can heal. And I believe this scandal in our Church must be woven into the fabric of today's broken yet beloved Church, woven with threads that spell out the names and that write the truth of those who have been sexually abused, exploited, used, harmed.

The Church will remain merely broken unless we listen to the voices of survivors. Unless we take action to condemn those who took our innocence away.

"What is due to the human being as a human being, and that means as a free entity, is first and foremost the acknowledgment of his or her human dignity," wrote Walter Kasper in his book *Mercy*:

> What is owed to every human being on the basis of his or her dignity is personal respect, personal acceptance, and personal care. In this sense, one can understand justice as the minimal measure of love and love as the full measure of justice.

Epilogue

In the updated April 30, 2023, Motu Proprio, *Vos Estis Lux Mundi*, "You are the light of the world," Pope Francis makes it clear that the responsibility of the Church is to give concrete witness of faith in Christ, both in our individual lives and in relationship with others, especially the successors of the Apostles, chosen by God to be leaders of his People. This means, those successors, the bishops, must do everything in their power to prevent and combat the crimes of sexual abuse in the Church— including combating their own abusive behavior and cover-ups. As Pope Francis writes:

> The crimes of sexual abuse offend Our Lord, cause physical, psychological and spiritual damage to the victims and harm the community of the faithful. In order that these phenomena, in all their forms, never happen again, a continuous and profound conversion of hearts is needed, attested by concrete and effective actions that involve everyone in the Church, so that personal sanctity and moral commitment can contribute to promoting the full credibility of the Gospel message and the effectiveness of the Church's mission. This becomes possible only with the grace of the Holy Spirit poured into our hearts, as we must always keep in mind the words of Jesus:
>
> Apart from me you can do nothing (John 15:5).
> Even if so much has already been accomplished, we

must continue to learn from the bitter lessons of the past, looking with hope towards the future.

As I understood it, this revised *Vos Estis Lux Mundi* Motu Proprio was part of an essential precursor to the Synod on Synodality with respect to the topic of the sexual abuse crisis across the global Church. And I believe it presents what the Synod on Synodality should bring forth to the Church about the scandal. A final report, approved by Pope Francis, is planned for release in 2025, a Jubilee year, which will be inaugurated on Christmas Eve, December 24, 2024, by Pope Francis as the Holy Year of 2025, titled *Pilgrims of Hope.*

As we go forth from 2025 with a new direction to imagine a different Church as the twenty-first century continues to unfold, there is much promise. My hope is the new direction will include abused pilgrims in the Church throughout the world. For them, justice, prevention, reconciled healing will only come by an unabashed announcement of truth to lead us all forward.

As the preparatory document, *Instrumentum Laboris,* summarizes the "characteristic signs of a synodal Church":

As a Church committed to listening, a synodal Church desires to be humble, and knows that it must ask for forgiveness and has much to learn. Some reports noted that the synodal path is necessarily a penitential one, recognising that we have not always lived the constitutive synodal dimension of the ecclesial community. The face of the Church today bears the signs of serious crises of mistrust and lack of credibility. In many contexts, crises related to sexual abuse, and abuse of power, money and conscience have pushed the Church to a demanding examination of conscience so that "moved by the Holy Spirit" the Church "may never cease to renew herself" (LG 9), in a journey of

repentance and conversion that opens paths of reconciliation, healing and justice.

The conclusion of the first session of the Synod on Synodality,
"For a Church That Listens and Accompanies," is stated in the
Summary Report *A Synodal Church in Mission*:

> The Church needs to listen with special care and sensitivity
> to the voices of victims and survivors of sexual, spiritual,
> economic, institutional, power and conscience abuse by
> clergy members or persons with Church appointments.
> Authentic listening is a fundamental element of the jour-
> ney toward healing, repentance, justice and reconciliation.

Be ready to work. But be heartened. In this critical period
in the life of the Church, there is no question that what Pope
Francis has orchestrated in his final years on earth by inviting
the people of God, all brothers and sisters, to imagine a different
Church through this Synod on Synodality is remarkable.

And, yes, the risks are high. The divisions within the current
Church have shaped discontent and significant mistrust. The
sexual abuse crisis has brought the Church to its knees. But
we can be restored. Broken, beautiful. Remade. The Church,
the gifts of the Church, the body of believers, the cross, and
the Eucharist are the gifts of God for the people of God. The
sacramental grace of our Lord, his flesh and blood, is ours. We
are loved by God, loved to live, and to be free—and to free each
other. The Holy Spirit is the one who mends, heals, and leads
with love.

And the Holy Spirit guides us in this time, calling those in
leadership positions in our Church to be open to change, to take
risks despite the fear of risk.

The risks are wider and more demanding—and more promising—when we listen, when we listen to those who are abused, when we listen to all of the voices in the Church, such as the voices of women religious. *"You can't listen to all the people of God,"* said Sr. Nathalie Becquart of the synod, *"if you don't listen to women and sisters. The entire synodal process has been to listen to each other and discern the Holy Spirit."*

Listen.

Jesus, at Lazarus's tomb, wept. The glory of God is ours when we wait together, cry together in darkness. When we wait, not in fear. But in listening, and in hope we will find the light.

"At the core of our existence, a transcendental neediness holds sway," wrote Johannes Baptist Metz in *Poverty of Spirit*. What holds sway for me is that we must discern. We must question. We must heal. We must agree to be Christ for one another. We must walk with him. And above all else, we must turn the rage of victims of sexual abuse in our Church into steps we take for changing the Church, so that the Church would be a vessel for healing and for peace.

In and out of the pews, abuse occurs everywhere. Sexually violated children, minors, and adult men and women, regardless of race, sexuality, economic status, ethnic background—all must discern how God brings comfort. When we, the abused, are accompanied by God and others in love, we more fully discover interior peace. We are all pilgrims, and living authentically depends on our ability, however broken we may feel, to rise again and again, not only for ourselves, but also for others who need us.

Field Hospital
Podcast Interview
with Mark Williams

Hosted by Jeannie Gaffigan and Mike Lewis,
April 27, 2022 (transcript excerpt)

Jeannie Gaffigan: Sexual abuse survivors have been wounded by the Church. Not only by the sick sexual predators that abused them, but also by the corrupt system that covered up their abuse to protect their own institution, leading to the abuse of more children. Catholics like us also betray survivors when we turn a blind eye to their plight, either because we don't want to deal with the trauma ourselves or we don't want to cause scandal. In my opinion, that makes us complicit in the culture of corruption. We have a responsibility to our Catholic brothers and sisters who are harmed in this.

Mike Lewis: We are extremely fortunate to have Mark join us on *Field Hospital,* because I think we have a lot to learn from him and his story. This is someone who has been able to use his own journey to help other survivors and to help the rest of us become advocates for survivors.

Jeannie: For the sake of our listeners, could you tell us a little bit about your journey? Only what you feel comfortable discussing from your early years, how you got to where you started to begin your healing?

Mark Joseph Williams: My father had just turned forty, when he died. And I had just turned twelve. I was a very vulnerable young man, young boy, really, at that point. My sister was three years younger than I. My mom suffered a lot of psychological illness and from alcoholism, and really went into a tailspin at that time. There were several men in my community and Church that reached out to her and to me. Some were well-intentioned; some were not, including a teacher who "groomed me." I was raped by him. At the time I was just thirteen and a half. About a year later, I was molested by a Roman Catholic priest. That molestation and relationship continued throughout my high school years. It was during that time of my adolescence that drinking became part of my life. . . . But for me, I was just caught up in it all and the early journey of addiction was something that really numbed all that pain. And removed me from it, really, which is very common with victims and survivors of sexual abuse. Back then, almost fifty years ago, there wasn't social media, so I was really alone. I was isolated. I was living in that pain that I wasn't even aware of, really. That's just the dynamic of abuse and the dynamic of being controlled, as it were. So that's the beginning of the story of what I went through. That early trauma that all these years later I now am able to name, which at the time was so crippling. . . . It really wasn't until I was arrested for the second time, driving while intoxicated, nearly twenty years ago in 2004, when I gave up the drink, cold turkey, and wound up being hospitalized.

There was a priest who visited me at this locked ward. I was on this locked ward for eight days. When I look back on it now, it really was God embracing me and saying to me, you really needed a time-out in your life.

I had a priest friend who was a real advocate for abuse victims and actually suffered terribly for his advocacy because of how the hierarchy treated him. But he was one of the early pioneers. I wasn't even in touch with what I had been through. But I was on that locked ward, and for some reason it was by the grace of God that I began to open up to him. Just a little bit. Told him a little more of what I had been through. And he had never known it. I'll never forget what he said to me: "This is your Gethsemane. This is your agony in the garden right now."

And that was the beginning of the healing. . . .

Jeannie: When did you decide that you were not only called to help other survivors to heal, but to work within and with Catholic leaders to heal the Church? Because that's the big thing for a lot of people: that the door is closed. So can I just ask you, how did you wind up helping people in the Church instead of saying, "I'm not going"?

Mark: One experience stands out the most in the last few years. The *New York Times* reached out to me because I had several letters published over the years, taking a position that the Church needed to do more. And I had written a few letters in support of Francis when I saw some of the things he was doing. But a couple of things happened. One was when he had to backtrack on Chile. I wrote a letter to Cardinal O'Malley, and I thanked him for really pushing Francis, who was his boss. O'Malley really spoke out and confronted Francis. I gave him a tremendous amount of credit for his courage. Then Francis invited some of the survivors from Chile to Rome. And we know what happened since. The other is that I was courageous enough to write Francis. And he wrote me back. He thanked me.

That gave me even more sense of conviction that I could be a voice in this Church. Then that summer, 2018, with the Pennsylvania grand jury report and the revelations of Theodore McCarrick in the parish that I used to belong to, there was a lot going on related to the abuse crisis and how the bishop—in a different diocese than the one I'm involved in now—was not handling it well. Things got triggered again for me. It's very common psychologically for triggers to happen again, so those events and the grand jury report on McCarrick shook me.

I met with the pastor. Asked him if I could come and see him. This is a man who was ordained by McCarrick, and he said to me—and I'll never forget—he said, "We all knew about him, but we couldn't say anything. We wanted to." And I knew right then and there that I was called to this parish.

A few weeks later, Cardinal Tobin, whom I had never met, was giving a talk at Fordham University on the inequality of the economy. This was in early September 2018, right after that whole summer of McCarrick and everything. When he preaches, Tobin always closes his eyes for maybe about thirty seconds. I think he just says a little prayer. And he opened his eyes, and he looked around the amphitheater, and said, "Tonight I come here with a very heavy heart." He said, "When I accepted this talk several months ago, the Pennsylvania grand jury report hadn't happened, and Theodore McCarrick hadn't happened. And I come here this evening asking for your prayers." He said: "I don't know what the answer is, but I know we can do better." I knew right then and there that I could help this man and the Church and his archdiocese do better. After the talk I made my way down to the stage, and our eyes met. I shook his hand and I said, "Cardinal, my name is Mark Williams and I'm a clerical abuse survivor. I would like to help you be part of the solution."

Mike: So, that's wonderful for Catholics; it's inspirational— that someone like you is willing to offer your time and your talent, expertise and experience, to help the Church. But every survivor story is different. Every case, of course, represents a failure from within the Church to protect the most vulnerable. And as we've discussed in the past, everyone's at a different stage in the healing process. Many people are angry at the Church.

You have remained Catholic. Your faith has actually grown in recent years.

But so many survivors have lost their faith. And they've left. Other survivors and advocates for survivors might see you as having become part of the system. How do you address this? You know those kinds of accusations, because I'm sure you've heard them when you're working with the Church, when you're talking with survivors, that skepticism.

Jeannie: And they've been burned. They've been burned many times. They've gone to the Church-appointed counselor. But then they get re-abused when they try to get help. So here you are trying to work with from within, but it immediately is going to cast some survivors away from you, saying, "Why were you working for them, the people who did this to us?"

Mark: Every victim/survivor has a different story, and he or she has been terribly affected by it, and many are not in the pews anymore. The only thing I can say is that I try to carry my message with the most sincere heart that I have. To your question, I'm not really working for them. I'm just carrying a message within them because I still believe that the Church is the solution. The Church that hurt me is also the Church that has helped. It's been the lifeline back to my life, my interior, the peace of my faith. And I think Francis has really helped me with that; forgiveness has helped me with that—and it's very hard to forgive a predator. Extraordinarily hard. I can't imagine everyone being able to do that. I can only say for myself that I have been given the real gift of grace to be able to do that. For my own health, for my own well-being. I really can't put into words what that kind of interior piece feels like, but I know it's a freedom. It's a real freedom.

I pray every day for victim/survivors across the world. Think about recent events in Germany and France, and all these independent commissions, the amount, the enormity of people. In some ways we're reliving it. And yet I've also been blessed with many good, holy priests who have been part of my life, who have been there for me. That's when I talk about the Church needing to listen to the victims, listen to the voices, so that they will really learn.

The Church is not perfect. That's from my corporate experience too. I've done a lot in my business life trying to help organizations improve. The human element is in every place, every family, every place of business. Sometimes it just ain't pretty that people really make mistakes. The Church is certainly leading the parade on that issue. But people like me and Juan Carlos Cruz and others, we need to raise the banner to help the Church heal, help the Church improve, and break the awful clericalism that's in the Church.

Jeannie: You know when you were talking about how the priest said, "We all knew." See, we all *didn't know.* So there was a huge reaction by people whose reaction was, wait a minute—*everything* I believed in is just this house of cards that is based on all these lies and clericalism and everyone covering each other's backs.

Mike: So here's the thing, what Jeannie said regarding not knowing about McCarrick: I live in the Archdiocese of Washington. So like you, I'm in the same region as where he once served, and I had heard the rumors during my more reactionary days. I sort of bought into them or subscribed to them. But then as I got older, I started thinking to myself that these rumors are so well known about the beach house. About McCarrick, about his proclivities. If it was true, surely the Church would have looked into this. Surely, they wouldn't have promoted him so many times. Surely, they wouldn't have named him a cardinal. And so when it came out in 2018, I'm not saying that I was entirely a victim. But I feel an injustice. We were more or less told, this is your archbishop; this is a person that you're supposed to respect. It was a betrayal. It was a betrayal to the Church.

So the thing that makes this crisis so terrible is that it's two crimes: not only is it the actual abuse and the abusers, but it is this cover-up or looking the other way by Church leaders.

Mark: I think the McCarrick report was certainly very telling. When you read all 467 pages of it, and Francis really was the one, I believe, who really drove that publication. When you read that report and you saw the clericalism at the very highest levels with John Paul II, Benedict XVI, and even a very conservative guy like Cardinal John O'Connor basically showing courage and letting them know what was going on. From a survivor's point of view, the one part of the report that is still an issue in the Church and still concerning is that the victims that were identified in that report, I think seven or eight of them, remained anonymous. Their names were not indicated in that report other than victim number one, two, three. And that's an issue in the Church, even though I give credit for those interviews to have happened and some of the things that were revealed. I really still believe that that perpetuates clericalism when you remain anonymous. . . . What Francis talks about in his letters was something that really convinced me that he is the "real deal" when he talked about creating a culture. Maybe this was the precursor to synodality. But he was talking about the "Me-Too" movement and about clericalism and about abuse, not only sexual, but of power and conscience, and he said, let us dream, creating that culture will take time, but it is an unavoidable commitment that we must make every effort to insist on. There must be no more abuse. Inside or outside of the Church. He went on to say that in the Church, there is a sense of entitlement, and that entitlement is the cancer of clericalism and the perversion of the vocation—very strong word—perversion of the vocation to which we priests are called. So he's identifying himself as a priest. He was so humble yet so strong in his message, and again for me, that helps me continue to dream and imagine a better Church.

Jeannie: There's the article that Mark wrote in the *New York*

Times, and I also want to just quote from it. Mark, you said, "People are leaving the pews in droves. No longer will the faithful embrace a hierarchical Church if those appointed to lead us fail to hold themselves and their fellow Cardinals and bishops to account. Abusers, regardless of their rank, must be removed from all ministerial activity."

That's very strong. Yeah. And you're not shy about it. It's not just that you're the yes man who says, Okay, I took a job with the Church. But let's keep this going and let's keep demanding accountability.

Mark: We're all instruments of faith. We're all channels of peace, and, as Francis says, and as is true in in many, many organizations, we need to get beyond this sense of entitlement that's at the heart of clericalism. And it's among some of these seminarians that I've experienced this. You could see the early signs of clericalism. I had the occasion recently to speak to a large group of seminarians. I asked, "Has anybody ever had occasion to have a conversation with a victim/survivor of clerical abuse?" Only one young man raised his hand. *Only one.* And when I was giving a virtual talk to the Jesuit provincials in Rome a few weeks later, only one-fourth of them reported having such a conversation. And these were very experienced men, who were running different regions of the world. Only *a quarter* of them had had an experience of having a conversation with a victim/survivor. Amazing. I didn't judge them all. I said, both to the seminarians and to those provincials taking the opportunity to listen: "To a survivor, the heart of Synodality is *listening.* That's my message."

Acknowledgments

Without the supportive, unabashed love of my bride, Karen, this book would not have been possible. For forty-five years, she has been by my side, and without her I would not be alive today. Our four children, Emily, Meryl, George, Rebecca, and their respective spouses, Ruddy, James, Kenia, Kasim, and our six grandchildren, Eve, Nessa, Aly, Grace, Amalia, and Benjamin, are truly gifts from God, and their lives have shaped mine in ways I can only describe with awe. The boundless love of my sister, Dawn Williams Harvey, has sustained me immeasurably. My sponsors and fellows in AA have been saints, men and women of such courage who have lifted me for the past twenty years of sobriety. This fellowship has taught me how to carry the message to another suffering alcoholic.

Another fellowship, that of victims/survivors of sexual abuse, is core to these pages and my life. Their vulnerability, strength, and advocacy for change in the Catholic Church, in the legal system, and for the protection of the rights of children has continued to hold me up—a stay against discouragement. I admire your bravery.

Many friends, living and of blessed memory, have accompanied me on my healing journey. An integral part of God's grace, they inspired me to put pen to paper. They include Msgr. George Deas, Cardinal Joseph Tobin, Fr. Dennis Berry, Msgr. Ken Lasch, Daniel Williams, MD, Joe Clemente, MD, David Taylor, MD, George Lombardi, MD, Sandy Davis, MD, Seth

Jerabek, MD, Deacon Bernie Nojadera, Dr. Jennifer Wortham, Mike Hoffman, Msgr. Jim Gotimer, Fr. John Unni, Msgr. Jack Carroll, Fr. Dan Murphy, Pastor Joel Biggers, James Martin, SJ, Tom Reese, SJ, Cardinal Sean O'Malley, Cardinal Blasé Cupich, Deacon Frank Owens, Deacon Ed Pluciniak, Deacon Ed Keegan, Deacon Jim Hackett, Deacon Rich Brady, Deacon Bill Ruane, Deacon Willy Malarcher, Bob Springer, SJ, Brother John Skates, Fr. Andy Prachar, Fr. Matthew Dooley, Fr. JC Merino, Msgr. Joseph Reilly, Professor Patrick Manning, Fr. Bill Rueger, Fr. Bruce Powers, Fr. Robert Lauder, Bishop Kevin Sweeney, Fr. Peter Garry, Bishop Elias Lorenzo, Bishop Michael Saporito, Bishop Manny Cruz, Bishop Gregory Studerus, Fr. John Chadwick, Fr. Benoit Alloggia, Tina Campbell, Sr. Donna Ciangio, Karen Clark, Gina Criscuolo, Larry Boland, Thomas Bistritz, Paul Donaldson, Bishop Brian McGee, Brian Devlin, Lou Monari, Herb Schneider, Bobby Zouvelous, Byron Gordon, Dr. Paul Zeitz, David Gibson, Peter Steinfels, Michel Plitt-Wirth, Maureen Meehan O'Leary, Paul Smith, Malcolm Scherz, John Brunner, Tom Welch, John Norcross, Brian Manning, Joe Kearney, Jack Kiley, John Murphy, Dave Pennella, Kevin Smith, Frank Seminara, Patrick O'Conner, Lou Palmeri, Neal Greene, Jerry Frech, Rick Diana, Ed McCarthy, Mark Newman, Patricia Williamson, Bob Hennelly, Ed Sapone, Fred Sosinsky, Patrick Brackley, Karen Livecchia, April Michelle Davis, Gina Bruno, Nancy Goodman Wells, Tad Jacks, Bishop James Johnston, Bishop Barry Knestout, Pat Clare, Tom Fuller, Mike Zedalis, Deacon Michael Montemurro, Gina Ferraioli, Dan Grossano, Marie Hack, Suzie Greco, Sara Dekker, Nadia Jamil, Maria Margiotta, Chris Jahn, Charlie Bryant, Bob Byrnes, Mary Jo Reid-Ebneth, Dennis Verbaro, Craig Siegel, Paul Dinter, Molly Fara, Archbishop Paul-Andre Durocher, Msgr. Robert Meyer, and many others who never left my side.

I am thankful to my early writing instructor, author Lauren

B. Davis, whose "Sharpening the Quill" classes for several years taught me how to sharpen my own quill. I am indebted to my dear friend Mike Lindemann who served as my unofficial editor and whose periodic surgical edits were invaluable well before I was fortunate to work with Orbis Books. Publisher Robert Ellsberg believed in this project from the get-go, and Lil Copan has been an expert eye in editing this book, helping my voice in ink become so much stronger. Others supported my work in different media: Mary Drohan with the *New York Times,* Baylis Greene with the *East Hampton Star,* Phil Garber with *Observer Tribune,* Paul Baumann with *Commonweal,* Kerry Weber with *America,* publishing letters and articles of mine over the years, words on the page that were precursors to this book. I am grateful to them for their commitment to publishing needed stories, including mine, related to trauma and sexual abuse in the Church.

I offer special gratitude to the faith communities whose parishioners have influenced my life: St. Patrick's, Chatham, NJ; St. Joseph's, Mendham, NJ; St. Matthew the Apostle, Randolph, NJ; and my home parish today, Church of the Little Flower, Berkeley Heights, NJ, located on the frontier in the Archdiocese of Newark (as Cardinal Tobin puts it). Over the past fifteen years, I have been blessed to attend several Cornerstone retreats. Some of those brothers who shared their own journeys include Jeff Boyer, Dave DiFusco, Pete Pasquale, Norm Hyman, John Carroll, Tom Galda, Rick Piovano, Prescott Schiables, John Fischer, Jose Montero, and Joe Sciortino. My healing story became clearer as I heard their stories. All have a story on the synodal road.

I am blessed to serve on the International Safeguarding Conference North American Working Group overseen by the USCCB as well as have the support of its members from the United States and Canada, who make up the conference. I am humbled to have the unwavering accompaniment of me as *survivor* by Fr. Hans Zollner, SJ, director of the Institute of

Anthropology, Interdisciplinary Studies on Human Dignity and Care, Pontifical Gregorian University, and, as well, the support of my fellow IADC Advisory Committee members from around the world dedicated to safeguarding in our Church; I am comforted by their commitment and ongoing support of countless victims in our midst.

During my writing *Torrent of Grace*, my dear friend, Mike Monahan, suffered a debilitating stroke. I pray for Mike every day and I know he continues to do the same for me even during his own moment of adversity. Beyond any question, God's love, His grace surrounds him and his family at this hour.

Finally, this book would never have seen the light of day without the wisdom of my trusted literary agent, Joseph Durepos. Nearly four and a half years ago, Joe and I became acquainted, and he was intrigued by my story. He kept saying to me, "Don't worry about a book, just keep doing what you're doing, the book will come, let it all evolve." Much has evolved, and when the time was right, the book was right. Joe believed people needed to hear how the same Church that hurt me could be a source for healing as well. His belief in sacramental grace echoed my own. And he helped me hold the belief that my story might resonate with others. As Henri Nouwen said, "What is most personal is most universal." Survivors can help heal other survivors—and the Church—when together we carry the cross and live in the same Spirit.

Selected Bibliography

XVI Ordinary General Assembly of the Synod of Bishops. *Instrumentum Laboris for the First Session of the 2021–2024 Synod: For a Synodal Church: Communication, Participation, and Mission.* Rome: October 28, 2023.

XVI Ordinary General Assembly of the Synod of Bishops. *A Synodal Church in Mission: Synthesis Report of the 16th Ordinary General Assembly of the Synod of Bishops.* Rome: October 28, 2023.

Albom, Mitch. *Tuesdays with Morrie.* London: Sphere, 2017.

Alcoholics Anonymous. *Alcoholics Anonymous: The Story of How Many Thousands of Men and Women Have Recovered from Alcoholism.* San Bernardino, CA: Alcoholics Anonymous World Services, 2018.

Alcoholics Anonymous. *Came to Believe.* New York: Alcoholics Anonymous World Services, 2014.

Alcoholics Anonymous. *Living Sober.* New York: Alcoholics Anonymous World Services, 2017.

Alcoholics Anonymous. *Twelve Steps and Twelve Traditions.* New York: Alcoholics Anonymous World Services, 2009.

Barron, Robert, and Word on Fire Catholic Ministries. *Letter to a Suffering Church: A Bishop Speaks on the Sexual Abuse Crisis.* Park Ridge, IL: Word on Fire, 2019.

Berg, Fr. Thomas. *Hurting in the Church: A Way Forward for Wounded Catholics.* Huntington, IN: Our Sunday Visitor, 2017.

Berg, Fr. Thomas, and Dr. Timothy Lock. *Choosing Forgiveness.* Huntington, IN: Our Sunday Visitor, 2022.

Bernardin, Cardinal Joseph. *The Gift of Peace: Personal Reflections.* New York: Image Books, 1998.

Brick, John, and Carlton K. Erickson. *Drugs, the Brain, and Behavior: The Pharmacology of Abuse and Dependence.* New York: Haworth Medical Press, 1999.

Brown, Raymond Edward, SS. *Priest and Bishop.* London: Burns & Oates, 1970.

Cahill, Thomas. *Pope John XXIII.* New York: Penguin, 2008.

Campisi, Roberto. Pope Francis Acknowledgment Letter, Office of Secretariat of State, Vatican, March 10, 2023.

Catechism of the Catholic Church. URBI et ORBI Communications: Rome, Italy. English translation for the United States of America copyright © 1994. United States Catholic Conference, Inc.—Libreria Editrice Vaticana.

Chittister, Joan. *The Breath of the Soul.* Hartford, CT: Twenty-Third Publications, 2009.

Chittister, Joan. *God's Tender Mercy: Reflections on Forgiveness.* New London, CT: Twenty-Third Publications, 2010.

De Ruiter, C., and Nancy Kaser-Boyd. *Forensic Psychological Assessment in Practice.* London: Routledge, 2015.

Devlin, Brian. *Cardinal Sin.* Dublin: Columba Books, 2021.

Dinter, Paul E. *The Other Side of the Altar.* New York: Farrar, Straus and Giroux, 2010.

Dulles, Avery, SJ. *The Resilient Church.* New York: Doubleday Books, 1977.

Eden, Dawn. *Remembering God's Mercy.* Notre Dame, IN: Ave Maria Press, 2016.

Ellsberg, Daniel. *The Doomsday Machine.* New York: Bloomsbury Publishing USA, 2017.

Ellsberg, Robert. *All Saints.* Chestnut Ridge, NY: Crossroad Publishing, 2013.

Erikson, Erik H. *Identity and the Life Cycle*. New York: Norton, 1959.

Felitti, V. J., R. F. Anda, D. Nordenberg, D. F. Williamson, A. M. Spitz, V. Edwards, M. P. Koss, J. S. Marks, "Relationship of Childhood Abuse and Household Dysfunction to Many of the Leading Causes of Death in Adults: The Adverse Childhood Experience (ACE) Study." *American Journal of Preventative Medicine* 14 (1998): 245–258.

Francis, Sergio Rubin, and Francesca Ambrogetti. *Pope Francis: Conversations with Jorge Bergoglio*. New York: G. P. Putnam's Sons, 2013.

Frankl, Viktor E. *Man's Search for Meaning*. Boston: Beacon Press, 1946.

Gibson, David. *The Coming Catholic Church*. New York: Harper Collins, 2011.

Goldstein, Dawn Eden. *Father Ed*. Maryknoll, NY: Orbis Books, 2022.

Greeley, Andrew M. *Life for a Wanderer*. New York: Doubleday, 1969.

Halík, Tomáš. *Touch the Wounds*. Notre Dame, IN: University of Notre Dame Press, 2023.

Heaton, Jean. *Helping Families Recover from Addiction*. Chicago: Loyola Press, 2020.

Herman, Judith Lewis. *Trauma and Recovery: Aftermath of Violence from Domestic Abuse to Political Terror*. New York: Basic Books, 2015.

Heschel, Abraham Joshua. *Quest for God*. Chestnut Ridge, NY: Crossroad, 1982.

Holiday, Ryan. *The Obstacle Is the Way: The Timeless Art of Turning Trials into Triumph*. New York: Portfolio/Penguin, 2014.

Hume, Basil. *To Be a Pilgrim: A Spiritual Notebook*. London: SPCK Press, 1988.

Imbelli, Robert P. *Rekindling the Christic Imagination*. Collegeville, MN: Liturgical Press, 2014.

Irish Jesuits. *Sacred Space*. Chicago: Loyola Press, 2023.

Ivereigh, Austen. *The Great Reformer*. New York: Henry Holt, 2014.

Jamison, Kay R. *An Unquiet Mind: A Memoir of Moods and Madness*. London: Picador, 1995.

Kasper, Cardinal Walter. *The Gospel of the Family*. Mahwah, NJ: Paulist Press, 2014.

Kasper, Cardinal Walter. *Mercy*. Mahwah, NJ: Paulist Press, 2014.

Kavanaugh, Kieran, OCD, and Otilio Rodriguez, OCD. *The Collected Works of Saint John of the Cross*. Washington, DC: Institute of Carmelite Studies, 1991.

Kennedy, Eugene. *Cardinal Bernardin's Stations of the Cross*. New York: St. Martin's Press, 2003.

Kolk, Bessel van der. *The Body Keeps the Score: Brain, Mind, and Body in the Healing of Trauma*. New York: Penguin Books, 2014.

Kushner, Harold S. *Living a Life That Matters: Resolving the Conflict between Conscience and Success*. New York: Alfred A. Knopf, 2001.

Lauder, Robert E. *Pope Francis' Spirituality & Our Story*. Totawa, NJ: Resurrection Press, 2014.

Lopez, Barry. *Winter Count*. New York: Vintage, 2010.

Manney, Jim. *What Matters Most and Why*. Novato, CA: New World Library, 2022.

Martin, James, SJ. *Building a Bridge: How the Catholic Church and the LGBT Community Can Enter into a Relationship of Respect, Compassion, and Sensitivity*. New York: HarperOne, 2018.

Martin, James, SJ. *Come Forth*. New York: HarperCollins, 2023.

Martin, James, SJ. *Jesus*. New York: HarperCollins, 2014.

Martin, James, SJ. *Learning to Pray: A Guide for Everyone.* San Francisco: HarperOne, 2022.

McBrien, Richard P. *Catholicism.* Vols. 1 and 2. New York: HarperCollins, 2013.

McNeill, John J. *The Church and the Homosexual.* Boston: Beacon Press, 2015.

Merton, Thomas. *Contemplation in a World of Action.* Garden City, NY: Doubleday, 1971.

Merton, Thomas. *Life and Holiness.* New York: Image Books Edition, 1964.

Merton, Thomas. *Love and Living.* London: Sheldon Press, 1986.

Merton, Thomas. *The Seven Storey Mountain.* New York: Harcourt, 1948.

Merton, Thomas. *Sign of Jonas.* New York: Image Books, 1955.

Metz, Johann Baptist. *Poverty of Spirit.* New York: Paulist Press, 1988.

Moore, R. L., ed. *Carl Jung and Christian Spirituality.* Mahwah, NJ: Paulist Press, 1988.

Moyers, Bill D. "A Gathering of Men with Robert Bly." Transcript. Billmoyers.com. Originally recorded January 8, 1990.

Moyers, William Cope, and Katherine Ketcham. *Broken: My Story of Addiction and Redemption.* New York: Penguin Books, 2007.

The New American Bible. Rev. ed. New York: Oxford University Press, 2004.

Newman, John Henry. *Lead, Kindly Light.* Orleans, MA: Paraclete Press, 1987.

Noceti, Serena. *Reforming the Church: A Synodal Way of Proceeding.* Mahwah, NJ: Paulist Press, 2023.

Nouwen, Henri J. M. *Community.* Maryknoll, NY: Orbis Books, 2021.

Nouwen, Henri J. M. *With Burning Hearts: A Meditation on the Eucharistic Life.* Maryknoll, NY: Orbis Books, 2003.

Nouwen, Henri J. M. *The Wounded Healer.* New York: Doubleday (An Image Book), 1979.

Nouwen, Henri J. M., and Robert Durback. *Seeds of Hope: A Henri Nouwen Reader.* London: Darton, Longman & Todd, 1998.

Parham, A. Philip. *Letting God.* Rev. ed. New York: HarperCollins, 1987.

Phillips, Donald T. *Lincoln on Leadership: Executive Strategies for Tough Times.* New York: Grand Central Publishing, 2009.

Plante, Thomas G., ed. *Sin against the Innocents: Sexual Abuse by Priests and the Role of the Catholic Church.* Westport, CT: Praeger, 2004.

Pope Benedict XVI (Joseph Cardinal Ratzinger), Stephan Otto Horn, and Vinzenz Pfnür. *God Is near Us: The Eucharist, the Heart of Life.* San Francisco: Ignatius Press, 2003.

Pope Benedict XVI (Joseph Cardinal Ratzinger). *God Is Love: Deus Caritas Est, Encyclical Letter.* Washington, DC: United States Conference of Catholic Bishops, 2006.

Pope Francis (Jorge Cardinal Bergoglio). *The Church of Mercy.* Chicago: Loyola Press, 2014.

Pope Francis (Jorge Cardinal Bergoglio). *Happiness in this Life.* New York: Random House, 2017.

Pope Francis (Jorge Cardinal Bergoglio). *The Joy of Gospel: Apostolic Exhortation Evangelii Gaudium of the Holy Father Francis to the Bishops, Clergy, Consecrated Persons and the Lay Faithful on the Proclamation of the Gospel in Today's World.* Erlanger, KY: Dynamic Catholic Institute, 2014.

Pope Francis (Jorge Cardinal Bergoglio). *On Fraternity and Social Friendship (Fratelli Tutti).* Maryknoll, NY: Orbis, 2020.

Pope Francis (Jorge Cardinal Bergoglio). *Vos Estis Lux Mundi— You Are the Light of the World.* Apostolic Letter promulgated May 9, 2019. [Replaced by Apostolic Letter published in *L'Osservatore Romano* effective April 30, 2023.]

Pope Francis (Jorge Cardinal Bergoglio) and Austen Ivereigh. 2020. *Let Us Dream*. New York: Simon and Schuster, 2020.

Pope Francis (Jorge Cardinal Bergoglio), Andrea Tornielli, and Oonagh Stransky. *The Name of God Is Mercy*. New York: Random House, 2016.

Pope John Paul II (Karol Cardinal Wojtyla). *Fruitful and Responsible Love*. New York: Seabury Press, 1979.

Rahner, Karl, SJ. *The Eucharist—The Mystery of Our Christ*. Denville, NJ: Dimension Books, 1970.

Robinson, Marilynne. *Gilead*. London: Virago, 2019.

Robinson, V. Gene. 2008. *In the Eye of the Storm*. New York: Church Publishing, 2008.

Rohr, Richard. *Breathing under Water: Spirituality and the Twelve Steps*. London: Society for Promoting Christian Knowledge, 2018.

Rohr, Richard. *Everything Belongs: The Gift of Contemplative Prayer*. New York: Crossroad, 2014.

Rohr, Richard. *Falling Upward: A Spirituality for the Two Halves of Life*. San Francisco: Jossey-Bass, 2013.

Rohr, Richard. *On the Threshold of Transformation: Soul Work for Men*. Chicago: Loyola Press, 2010.

Rohr, Richard. *The Universal Christ: How a Forgotten Reality Can Change Everything We See, Hope for, and Believe*. New York: Convergent Books, 2019.

Rolheiser, Ronald. *The Holy Longing: The Search for a Christian Spirituality*. New York: Doubleday, 1999.

Rolheiser, Ronald. *The Shattered Lantern: Rediscovering a Felt Presence of God*. New York: Crossroad, 2004.

Saul, Jack. *Psychotherapy Networker*. September–October 2023.

Secretariat of State of the Holy See. *Report on the Holy See's Institutional Knowledge and Decision-Making Related to Former Cardinal Theodore Edgar McCarrick (1930–2017)*. Vatican City State, 2020.

Sheveland, John N. *Theology in a Post-Traumatic Church*. Maryknoll, NY: Orbis Books, 2023.

Steinfels, Peter. *A People Adrift: The Crisis of the Roman Catholic Church in America*. New York: Simon & Schuster, 2004.

Styron, Alexandra. *Reading My Father: A Memoir*. New York: Scribner, 2012.

Styron, William. *Darkness Visible: A Memoir of Madness*. London Vintage, 2009.

Tobin, Cardinal Joseph W., CSsR. "A Synodal Church Is the Solution to the Sexual Abuse Crisis: 20 Years after the Dallas Charter." Address to USCCB General Assembly, November 15, 2022.

Tutu, Desmond, and Mpho Tutu. *The Book of Forgiving*. New York: HarperCollins, 2014.

United States Conference of Catholic Bishops (USCCB). *The Power of Forgiveness: Pope Francis on Reconciliation*. Newark, NJ: Ascension Press, 2021.

Vatican Council II: The Conciliar and Post-Conciliar Documents, ed. Austin Flannery, OP. New rev. ed. Northport, NY: Costello, 1992.

"Way of the Cross Prayer Service." From Awake, A Community of Abuse Survivors, Concerned Catholics, and Allies Responding to the Wounds of Sexual Abuse in the Catholic Church. Lent 2023. www.awakecommunity.org.

Wijlens, Myriam, and Vimal Tirimanna, CSsR, eds. *The People of God Have Spoken: Continental Ecclesial Assemblies with Synod on Synodality*. Dublin: Columba Books, 2023.

Williams, Daniel T., MD. In *Merritt's Neurology*, ed. Lewis P. Rowland, MD, 11th ed., New York: Columbia University Press, 2005.

Williams, Mark. "Reflections with Mark Williams," in conjunction with Joseph Cardinal Tobin's address to USCCB General Assembly, November 15, 2022

Williams, Mark Joseph, interview by Mike Lewis and Jeannie Gaffigan. *Field Hospital* podcast, transcript. US Catholic, sponsored by The Valitorians, April 27, 2022.

Wilson, George B., SJ. *Clericalism: The Death of the Priesthood*. Collegeville, MN: Liturgical Press, 2017.

Woititz, Janet G. *Adult Children of Alcoholics*. New York: Simon and Schuster, 2010.

Wortham, Jennifer. *A Letter to the Pope*. New York: New Insights Press, 2018.

Yalom, Irvin D. *The Gift of Therapy*. London: Piatkus, 2002.

Permissions
and Sources

I have taken care to protect confidentiality and individual privacy in stories in this book about the recovery and experience of individuals regarding sexual abuse, including those related to forensic legal work with incarcerated persons.

Personal stories shared with me in conversation, emails, letters by a variety of individuals, including my peers in Alcoholics Anonymous, lawyers, and incarcerated individuals, are used by express permission of those individuals and/or their legal representatives. Some names have been omitted entirely, while others have been changed or reduced to first names only. Names, including full names, have been used only when that individual explicitly requested such. Where individuals mentioned have shared materials and requested their names be changed or only first names used, I have done so.

All Alcoholics Anonymous materials are copyright of Alcoholics Anonymous World Services, copyright © 2009, 2014, 2017, and 2018.

Chapter 2: Tour of Duty

Child abuse statistics are taken from World Health Organization, https://www.who.int. Used by permission.

Additional studies and information can be found at: The Global Collaborative, www.globalcollaborative.org.

The author's forensic interview with "Lawrence" is cited with his permission as communicated by his family.

Chapter 4: Clerical Silence

"Sister B:" Letter to Pope Benedict XVI, and her exchange with the author, were translated by Fr. Christian Staedter of the Archdiocese of Paderborn (Germany) and are used with permission.

Chapter 5: A Violation Thwarted

"Erika:" Story based on conversation with the author and reproduced with permission.

Chapter 7: Decent into Hell

Mike Hoffman's email to the author is reproduced with his permission.

Chapter 8: Locked Ward

The author's conversation with Monsignor Kenneth Lasch is cited with permission.

Chapter 10: Gentle Expert

The author's consultation with Daniel T. Williams, MD, and quotations from Dr. Williams are used with permission.

Chapter 12: The Truth Will Out

Quotation from AA peer, Mark K., was emailed to the author and is used with permission.

The author's daughter, Rebecca, is quoted with permission.

Chapter 13: From Victim to Surviror

The email from the author's friend Deborah is reproduced with her permission.

Chapter 14: A Friendship Is Born

This account of the author's friendship with Joseph Cardinal Tobin is included with his permission.

Chapter 15: Accompaniment and Hope in Francis

Mark Joseph Williams, Address to USCCB General Assembly, November 15, 2022, and Joseph Cardinal Tobin, Address to USCCB General Assembly, November 15, used by permission of Office of the General Counsel, USCCB.

Excerpts from the November 15, 2022 Plenary Session copyright © 2022, United States Conference of Catholic Bishops, Washington, DC. All rights reserved.

Chapter 16: The Way of the Cross and the Eucharist

Dr. Jennifer Wortham's letter to Pope Francis is quoted by permission.

"Way of the Cross Prayer Service." From Awake, A Community of Abuse Survivors, Concerned Catholics, and Allies Responding to the Wounds of Sexual Abuse in the Catholic Church. www.awakecommunity.org, Lent, 2023. Used by permission of Sara Larson, executive director, who in turn obtained permission from each of the individual participants in the service.

Chapter 17: Walking the Synodal Road

The conversation with Fr. Hans Zollner, SJ, is cited with his permission.

Field Hospital Podcast Interview with Mark Williams

Excerpts from transcript of Mark Joseph Williams interview by Mike Lewis and Jeannie Gaffigan. *US Catholic*, sponsored by The Valitorians, April 27, 2022. Used by permission.